Dan Juster is a significant voice th
today. Through the lenses of Chur
provides sound Biblical understan
direction of the church. I especially
seeking to better understand the in
relationship with Israel as it relates
into all that God has called her.

Mike Bickle
Executive Director
Friends of the Bridegroom

In a day where authentic unity in the Church is so desperately needed,
That They May Be One is a breath of fresh air. In this overview of Church
history, Dan Juster explains how the Church's attitude toward Israel
and a more Biblical understanding of her Jewish roots provide very
significant keys for releasing greater measures of unity within the Body
of Christ.

Larry Kreider
International Director
D.O.V.E. Christian Fellowship International

Dan Juster is a voice — a forerunner — helping to prepare the Body
of Messiah to be all we are called to be. With a deep commitment to
theological integrity and the power of the Spirit, Dan is providing vital
leadership in this crucial hour. This book will serve to help bridge the
gap between Jew and Gentile, and aid us in moving together as one new
man in Yehsua.

Robert Stearns
Executive Director
Eagles' Wings

Through this Messianic perspective of Church History, Dan Juster shares
how a greater understanding of the Church's Jewish roots provides a more
accurate awareness of her identity as a partner with God in His purposes
being released in the earth. *That They May Be One* wonderfully puts into
focus the importance of Israel and the Jewish roots of the Church for a
greater self-awareness of every believer in the Body of Christ.

Don Finto
Senior Pastor
Belmont Family of Churches

Other Books by Author

Jewish Roots
A Foundation of Biblical Theology

The Irrevocable Calling
Israel's Role As A Light to the Nations

Jewishness and Jesus

Relational Leadership
A Manual of Leadership Principles for Congregational Leaders and Members

Growing to Maturity
A Messianic Jewish Guide

Dynamics of Spiritual Deception

The Biblical World View
An Apologetic

Due Process
A Plea for Biblical Justice Among God's People

Israel, the Church, and the Last Days

Revelation
The Passover Key

That They May Be One

Printed in the United States of America

Cover Design by
Josh Huhn, DesignPoint, Inc.
Layout Design by
Valerie Levy, Drawing Board Studios
Edited by
Elisa Laird, Red Pen Resources

12 11 10 09 4 3 2 1

ISBN 978-880226-71-1

Library of Congress Catalog Control Number: 2009931815

Lederer Books
A division of
MESSIANIC JEWISH PUBLISHERS
6120 Day Long Lane
Clarksville, MD 21029

Distributed by
Messianic Jewish Resouces International
Order line: (800) 410-7367
E-mail: Lederer@messianicjewish.net
www.messianicjewish.net

That They May Be One

A Brief Review of Church Restoration Movements and their Connection to the Jewish People.

(formerly One People, Many Tribes)

Daniel C. Juster Th.D.

Lederer Books
A division of Messianic Jewish Publishers
Clarksville, Maryland

CONTENTS

Introduction

Understanding Church History

Having spent thirty-five years in the Messianic Jewish movement, I have heard many views among Messianic Jews concerning the Christian Church. I have also seen an amazing variety of views from Christians concerning Jews, Judaism, and Messianic Jews. Some in the Messianic community think the Church is pagan because it does not celebrate the right feast days. Some Christians think that Judaism is an aberration and even that Jewish people are no longer benefactors of God's promises. Those of us in Messianic Judaism must understand the Church with a balanced perspective recognizing the Jewish connection. This, in turn, will be a positive step toward helping Christians correctly understand Jews and Messianic Jews.

A healthy understanding of the Church is vital for those Jews and Gentiles who are part of the Messianic Jewish community. We, as the restored remnant of Israel, are not going to be able to fulfill our task if we are not in a positive relationship with the Church. This includes not only individuals, but also our relationship to the corporate expressions of the Church.

A correct understanding of Messianic Judiasm is also important for all Christians. To not recognize what God is doing among his chosen people is to miss his program for the world. As this age moves to its closing drama, a Jewish perspective on Church history is past due so that we can fulfill our mutual destiny, together.

This book is not just a brief summary of Church history. It is history with a perspective—one that shows the connection to the Jewish people. I trust that this book will be helpful to all who read it.

within ?

What Is the Meaning of History?

How history is examined depends on if history is viewed as being purposeful or merely a collection of successive events and facts that show historical causation but no significant larger purpose. The latter view, held by most secular historians, provides an understanding of human individual and corporate behavior and may provide direction for future nations, especially given their present challenges. Yet, in this view, interpretation comes only from a worldly perspective.

In the biblical view, however, God is the Lord of history. The center of history is found in God's involvement with it. The center of God's action in history is Israel and the Church. Consider the principle of sowing and reaping. Nations, not only individuals, act in ways that over time result in consequences that alternately enhance or destroy humanity. In this framework, history takes on a whole different interpretation; it teaches us lessons about God's ways.[1] The most profound historical writing is the history of Israel and the Church found in Numbers, Kings, Chronicles, the Gospels and Acts. In the Bible, history is understood from the perspective of what God is seeking to do through the ages.

But by what criteria should we evaluate cultures that are not directly a part of the biblical narrative? The answer is found in the revelation given through Noah. What nations do with the truths revealed to Noah determines their quality of life. All nations are descended from Noah, and most cultures have some memory of the fall and flood. The writings of Theodore Gaster on world mythologies and many other writings give evidence of this this lingering Noahic memory.[2]

---

[1]   I believe that the primary reason many people view history as a boring topic is because it has often been taught as a collection of mere facts. History never was to be taught this way.

[2]   Not all cultures do, but most regions of the world do. There was revelation that came down to the human race from Noah. Most nations and cultures repudiate that revelation or allow that revelation to be perverted.

After Noah, God chose a people—the Nation of Israel—to restore and extend his truth to the other nations. Israel was the keeper of this revelation and the source through which God would turn the world back to himself. History is the story of God's redemption. Biblically, Israel has yet to restore God's truth throughout the world. After Yeshua returns to the Earth, the Kingdom of God will expand in fullness from Israel to the nations of the world,[3] paralleling the Kingdom's advancement in partial form from Israel to the nations in the early centuries of Church history.

Putting history into this broader context of sowing (God's revelation sown among the nations) and reaping (the fruit of what the nations have done with this revelation) indicates that history is God's story of what the world has done and is doing with the Gospel. It is also the story of what the world has done with the Noahic revelation and God's revelation through nature (Rom. 1). These elements form the center of our theory of history.

---

[3]   Discernment is needed to interpret history, specifically about the direction of the nations that have not heard the Gospel in contrast to those nations that have. What have the nations that have heard the Gospel done with the opportunity given to them?

I

New Covenant History

The book of Acts gives a historic beginning in the midst of the earth's story. It was not new in regard to birthing the people of God because Israel was already corporately God's chosen people. However, not every individual in Israel was saved.

In Acts, the apostles embrace the New Covenant. They plant a new community with a new revelation. It is important to understand this new "apostolic perspective" in launching the body of believers, which came to be known as the "Church."[1]

The center of history became the *kehillah* ('congregation' in Aramaic or Hebrew) of Yeshua.

> "Upon this rock[2] I will build my [*kehillah*] congregation; and the gates of hell shall not prevail against it" (Matt. 16:18 KJV).

The disciples did not understand the implications of what Yeshua was saying in this verse in Matthew. He was creating a people from all of the world's nations that would be a manifestation of his Kingdom.

The terminology used in the body of believers today is so skewed that we do not see the importance of what Yeshua said. Even the phrase "go to church" or the question, "Where

---

[1] Throughout this book the terms body of believers and Church will be used interchangeably.
[2] I interpret "the rock" to be the confession of Yeshua's kingship, or the confession of his Messiahship, because he is the king of the Kingdom of God. He is the king that rules on the Davidic throne.

do you go to church?" is an unbiblical way of speaking that blinds us to the meaning of this verse. We do not "go to church." We *are* the Church. We go to the corporate body's expression of the worship. We go to a meeting for teaching and to be equipped by the leadership of that corporate body. The fact that the word *church* has its true background in the word *kehillah* shows us how skewed our terminology is. Replace the word *church*, which also refers to a building, with *congregation*. The question, "Where do you go to church," continues the misunderstanding. The right question is, "What community or congregation are you a part of?"

Let us look at the meaning of this new reality Yeshua brought into being.

The Disciples' Understanding of God's Plan

Let us begin our discussion with Matthew 16 where Yeshua declared that he would "establish his congregation and the gates of hell would not prevail against it." In regard to leadership in this new community, Yeshua tells Peter that he is given the keys of the Kingdom. This is extended to the disciples in general in Matthew 18 because the keys have to do with the power of binding and loosing according to rabbinic thought. The doctrine of the keys refers to the authority to make judicial decisions in Israel. Matthew 18:18 speaks of this judicial authority in these terms: "Whatever you bind on earth will be bound in heaven." This means that they had the authority to decide what practices people were loosed from and bound to. It also referred to a judicial penalty that had to be accepted by the rest of the community. Before this time, God limited that kind of authority to the judges in Israel with the ultimate judges being the Sanhedrin, the supreme court of Israel. After the destruction of Jerusalem and the elimination of the Sanhedrin, rabbinic writers claimed that this authority passed to them.

When Yeshua said, "I will establish my congregation and the gates of hell will not prevail against it," the disciples likely thought, *There's going to be a synagogue within Israel! It's going to be strong, and we will have strong authority in it. It will eventually take over the nation.* Their perspective, given in Matthew 16, was that Yeshua was transferring the authority from the Sanhedrin to them indicated by Yeshua's giving them the keys of the Kingdom. After Yeshua died on the cross and was resurrected, the disciples came to a fuller understanding of what this transference of authority meant. At first their Messiah's death shocked them because they had thought that he was going to fulfill the prophecies to deliver Israel from foreign oppression. They had hoped that this glorious deliverance would bring the Age to Come[3] in fullness. Instead, Yeshua had been crucified. They had been stunned. Then three days later he had been resurrected, and they had been overcome with joy.

He taught his disciples for forty days, and yet even then they still did not understand everything. Forty days passed, and Yeshua appeared to his disciples on the Mount of Olives. It is very important that we are able to see this passage differently. They said, Will you at this time restore the Kingdom to Israel? In other words, "Will you at this time do what the Messiah is supposed to do—deliver us from the Romans, bring that glorious deliverance the prophets spoke of, and then bring the Kingdom Age come fullness?"

The disciples did not yet understand that Yeshua was bringing the Kingdom in part so that its expression was in the healed lives of believers, through the quality of love and justice practiced within the congregations of Yeshua. We are to create communities of love and justice in the way we treat each other, and we are to enforce the standards of God.

Contrary to what is taught in many sectors of the Church, Yeshua did not say or imply, "Don't you understand that I'm not going to do that? I'm here to bring in a spiritual kingdom. I'm not here to bring an external worldwide millennial kingdom; your theology is wrong; you're still thinking carnally.

---

[3]   The Age to Come refers to the time where all things in heaven and earth are restored to their proper place and function. This will occur after Yeshua returns the second time to the earth to set up his physical earthly reign together with the Church, his bride.

You've got to be more spiritual." Such teaching is simply out of context and untrue. Yeshua said, "It is not for you to know the times or the seasons." The issue was timing and not their view of a literal kingdom.

Yeshua's answer can be interpreted in this way, "Yes, what you're expecting is right. It is going to come but not yet. You cannot know when the final act will come. First, you must go to Jerusalem and there wait for the promise of the Father. You are going to receive power after the Holy Spirit comes on you, and then you are going to become witnesses—first in Jerusalem, Judea, Samaria, and then to the uttermost parts of the earth" (Acts 1:8). After that, Yeshua was taken up into the heavens, and the disciples were amazed. An angel appeared and said, "Why stand you gazing up into heaven? This same Yeshua whom you have seen will come again in like manner as you have seen Him go" (Acts 1:11).

The disciples had no idea that Yeshua's return would take two thousand-plus years! So the last instruction they had was to go to Jerusalem and wait. They went and waited, and a wonderful miracle took place. The Spirit was poured out on 120 faithful disciples. They spoke in other languages. There was a great rush of wind, and tongues of fire seemed to rest upon them all. They went out onto the street and preached the Good News to the Jewish people who had gathered from all over the world for the Feast of *Shavuot* (the Feast of Pentecost). Thousands responded. Remember that these people were now gathered in Jerusalem and were mostly Jews who spoke different languages because they resided in different countries. There were also proselytes among the Gentiles.

The Disciples' Understanding Grows

We can imagine at this point what the disciples thought about eschatology (an understanding of how history would develop at the end of the age). *Well, of course, before he overthrows the Romans, we've got to get Israel to repent! Now, we understand!* Well, they understood—partially. They believed that once Israel accepted Yeshua as the Messiah-King, the Romans would be overthrown and then the Kingdom would fully arrive.

Did you ever ask yourself why there is no recorded mission to the Gentiles in the first ten chapters of the book of Acts? Yeshua taught, "You will receive power after the Holy Spirit comes upon you, and you will be my witnesses in Jerusalem, Judea, Samaria, and to the uttermost parts of the earth." They probably thought, *We've got to share what we have seen and heard with the Jewish people in the Diaspora, the Jews all over the world.* They weren't thinking of Jerusalem, Judea, and Samaria as places to share this with the Gentiles; they were only thinking about the Jews! They did, however, share the Gospel with the Samaritans but only after a scattering from persecution (Acts 8).

In Matthew 28:19, Yeshua said, "Therefore go and make disciples of all nations... " Obviously the disciples did not understand Jesus' words. Perhaps their thinking was, *Of course, we'll disciple all of the nations when Yeshua returns. After Israel has repented and been delivered, then we'll go out and disciple all of the nations.* They put Yeshua's words in the framework of a first-century Jewish understanding of how history would develop. They were looking forward to Israel repenting, after which they were expecting the Messiah to come. In Acts 3:19–21, Peter said to an all Jewish audience, "Repent that God might send Yeshua, who must remain in heaven until the times of the restoration of all things (Age to Come) spoken by the mouth of all his holy prophets since the world began." He must remain in heaven *until* the times of the restoration. That *until* is connected to Israel's repenting and receiving him corporately as the messianic king.[4]

Within the framework of first-century Judaism, the disciples probably reasoned, Mission to the Gentiles? Why would we want to do that? All we have to do is get Israel saved, and

---

[4]   Messiah is a more accurate translation than Christ because it implies a kingly rule on David's throne. I don't think the term Christ conveys what Messiah conveys— even in the English language. The word Messiah literally means "anointed" (king or ruler on David's throne). Was Christ the divine side while Jesus was the human side? No. This is wrong theology, but that's how many Christians often think.

then, of course, the nations will all come to the truth! The Hebrew Bible in text after text declares that Israel's restoration will lead to the salvation of the nations. The blinders over the minds of the nations will be removed when Israel fully embraces Yeshua. They might have thought of texts like Isaiah 25, which said the blindness of the nations would be removed.

God's Plan for the Age

The disciples were in for a big surprise on two fronts. First, they had no idea at this time that they had a mission to the Gentiles. Second, they had no idea that Israel would say, "No!" to their preaching of the Good News. They had the testimony of the Resurrection. They had the empty tomb. They had signs and wonders like the world had never seen. They probably figured it was only a matter of time—even a brief period of time—until all Israel would believe. I believe that part of the reason the disciples were unable to understand what Yeshua was saying was because they did not fully understand Daniel 9.

My understanding of Daniel 9 is different than dispensationalism, where believers are taken from the earth seven years before Yeshua's return to earth. Also, I believe that the one who confirms the covenant in verse 27 is the Messiah (not the Antichrist). Yeshua validated the covenant during the three and a half years of his ministry. Then, the disciples continued its verification in Jerusalem for another three and a half years (the period from Pentecost to the first great persecution and scattering). These two periods total seven years.

In the midst of the seventieth week, the seventieth period of seven years (Daniel 9;24-27) Yeshua died and ended oblation in the sense that the sacrifices lost their centrality and were no longer effective. Apostolic preaching confirmed the covenant for the last half of the seventieth week, and then judgment fell as evidenced in the Talmud. According to the Talmud, the doors of the Temple swung open during the days of Johanan ben Zakkai, a rabbi during the Second Temple Period, signifying that judgment was coming. It also records that after *Yom Kippur* (Day of Atonement), the cord outside of the Temple no longer turned from red to white as an indication of the sacrifices' acceptance.[5] The Talmud places this event in Jerusalem in 30 C.E., the approximate year of Yeshua's death and forty years before the Temple was destroyed. Then, Titus, the prince, came and destroyed the city and the sanctuary as mentioned in verse 26. God allowed one generation, forty years of mercy, before the actual judgment fell.

The disciples probably believed that Israel would accept their witness. However, the prediction of the Temple's destruction in Daniel 9 and Yeshua's predictions of Jerusalem's and the Temple's destruction implies that Israel would reject their witness. I think the disciples still believed that Israel would be delivered from Roman domination after she completely accepted Yeshua. Then, Yeshua would return and the nations would come to faith. Yet this does not fit Daniel 9, which implies that Israel would reject the covenant after seven years. Though unforeseen by the disciples, the mission to the Gentiles would become a key to Israel's salvation. All of this fits with my interpretation of the time of the covenant's confirmation in Daniel 9.

But before that happened, the disciples found that most of the religious leaders did not accept the miracle of Yeshua's resurrection. If they had accepted the Resurrection, what would have happened? They would have had to submit to the apostles' authority because the keys of the Kingdom had been given to them. Rather than choose that option, Israel's leaders led her astray. Only a remnant, a large minority in this case, believed. The remnant who believed, and that number was growing, now were handed an unanticipated part of the puzzle. They never dreamed of a united community of Jew and Gentile that would be the bride of the Messiah before Israel was delivered. This was key to Israel's believing, being

---

[5] Babylonian Talmud, Yoma 39b, "During the last forty years before the destruction of the Temple... the crimson-colored strap [did not] become white." See also Rosh Hashanah 31b.

re-engrafted, and being delivered from her oppressors. This is Paul's teaching, which notes that this new community will make Israel jealous so that she might be re-engrafted (Rom. 11:11–15).

In Romans 11:11 Paul made an astounding statement, "Salvation has come to the Gentiles for the purpose of making Israel jealous!" Yet at the same time, Paul, a Jew, said, "I magnify my ministry, if by any means I may provoke to jealousy those who are of my flesh and save some of them." As a representative of Israel's saved remnant, he is speaking to the body of gentile believers and saying that they are to follow his example in making Israel jealous. This implies that they, both Jewish and gentile believers, make Israel jealous. Then and only then will Israel be grafted back in. When the chosen people turn to Yeshua, the mighty deliverance will come so that Peter's words will be fulfilled, "Repent...that God may send Yeshua!" (Acts 3:19–20).

Did Paul know of Peter's teaching? He very possibly did because Luke, who wrote these words, was his traveling companion. However, whatever the state of Paul's knowledge, his writings harmonize with Peter's message. The return of Yeshua is still contingent, I believe, on Jewish repentance.

And Paul says that the key to bringing Israel to faith in Yeshua is the Church and its rich, enigmatic relationship with the Holy Spirit. This mystery was not previously seen by the prophets (Eph. 2, 3), and plays several functions in this world. We need to understand the Church's functions to understand the mystery. When we grasp the great calling God has for the Church, we see how the Church falls short of her faith.

First, the body of believers is to be a manifestation in this age of the Age to Come. How does that happen? The Age to Come is realized in the present time by the gifts and the power of the Holy Spirit in us. Hebrews 6:5 states that we who have tasted of the Holy Spirit have tasted of the Age to Come. In the Age to Come, Israel and the nations will be one under the rule of the Messiah. In this age, Jew and Gentile are one under the rule of Messiah in the body of believers.

Second, the body of believers extends the Kingdom of God to all of the nations. Those who respond before the very end of this age and the awesome judgments and wrath of God are poured out have the privilege to be part of the bride. Jew and Gentile who respond in this age will be the ruling queen by his side in the Age to Come.

Third, in extending the Kingdom to the nations, a people is formed in the midst of the Earth who have power in intercession and in witness to do what even the apostles could not do—to turn Israel back to Yeshua. Then all of the prophecies of the Age to Come will be fulfilled. The body's purpose is to preach and live the power and fullness of the Kingdom's Gospel as a witness to the entire world and to make Israel jealous. When this task is fulfilled, Yeshua will return. When will this happen? No one knows, but I pray it's soon.

The role of the Church is not secondary in regard to the role of Israel. Many Christians are upset with those who emphasize Israel because they think it means that Christians are inferior. However, every believer is the spiritual seed of Abraham, raised with Yeshua, and seated with Yeshua in heavenly places (Eph. 2:6). There is no inferiority—ever! There is simply a call for Israel to be the capital nation in the midst of all of the earth's nations in the Age to Come.

The Church finds its purpose and meaning rooted in Israel. God revealed this to the apostles, especially to Paul. James got a partial revelation that the Gospel was to be extended to the Gentiles (Acts 15). He quoted Amos 9, saying that if the Holy Spirit was poured out already, then why can't Jew and Gentile become one before the Age to Come arrives in fullness? The apostles always saw the body of believers as something Jewish in roots, purpose, and constitution.

The Commonwealth of Israel

The apostles saw the body of believers as the commonwealth of Israel, not a replacement of the nation proper but a commonwealth like the British commonwealth in the days of its actual rulership (Eph. 2:12). They saw that the commonwealth is not completed until the saved remnant grows to the point that the whole nation of Israel comes to faith in Yeshua. Then in the Age to Come, all nations will make up the commonwealth of Israel, ruled by Yeshua and his queen—the body of believers who embraced Yeshua before the Second Coming. That's the total commonwealth that God is after.

Does the Church supersede Israel as taught in replacement theology? In other words, does the Church take Israel's place as God's people? Yes and no. Yes, in the sense that those who are Yeshua's followers receive the fullness of New Covenant benefits and those of Israel who do not believe in Yeshua presently do not have the fullness of those benefits. Jews who do not believe in Yeshua are spoken of as the olive tree's broken-off branches (Rom. 11:17–24). The answer is also a resounding no in the sense that Israel is still chosen, kept, and preserved as God's chosen one and will one day be fully and corporately re-engrafted into the commonwealth of God, which the olive tree represents, believing Jews and Gentiles in one body. The commonwealth viewpoint represents the bigger picture. So, yes, the body of believers—made up of Jew and Gentile—is the place of primary New Covenant blessing now, but Israel is preserved by biblical promise and destined to corporate or national re-engrafting.

By the end of the Second Temple Period,[6] the apostles had this understanding. They grasped their role in relation to Israel and the larger Church. They knew there were distinct callings for Jew and Gentile. The members of the commonwealth are not called to come under all aspects of Israel's distinctive calling. Acts 15 implies that the nation proper maintains its distinct calling. As I argue in my book *The Irrevocable Calling*, this is the fullness of Torah life given to Israel and a pictorial manifestation of important truths. The Gentiles were exempt from the obligations of Jewish life but not from a respect for Jewish identity and practice, which is a Jewish priestly calling

---

6   The end of the Second Temple Period is 70 C.E. when Titus destroyed the Temple.

that benefits all. In Acts 21, we read that the Jews were still zealous for the Law and there is no condemnation of them. But in Acts 15, the Gentiles are only enjoined to keep the parts of the Law that are more universal as reflected in New Covenant Scripture and in what rabbis later called the Noahide commandments—not eating meat sacrificed to idols, fornication, eating animals that were strangled, and eating blood—given through Noah to all people. They are not responsible to live out the picture that Israel lives before the nations. Gentiles are also free to join Jewish people in celebrations of the feasts but again are not expected to keep these days as a matter of covenant responsibility.[7]

My perspective is that God is moving to bring the body of believers to a place of completeness and maturity whereby she will be able to fulfill her role of making Israel jealous. This envy is the ultimate victory of the body. To accomplish this, the Gospel of the Kingdom has to be proclaimed. Israel must see that the body of believers are a people who fulfill Yeshua's John 17 prayer, ". . . [T]hat they might be one... that the world might believe." We know that the world won't believe until the millennial age. The knowledge of the Lord will then cover the earth as the waters cover the sea (Isa. 11).

Part of what will bring the millennial age is the unity, or oneness, of the body of believers. This oneness includes holiness, maturity and doctrine.[8] Yeshua prayed that they might be one as the Father and Yeshua are one (John 17:22–23).

---

[7]   Gentile is not a pejorative or negative term. It is literally an abbreviation for nations—those from among all nations. The word is used so Paul doesn't have to say, "I want to speak to you Frenchmen, Romans, Chinese, and Japanese." It would take too long. Gentiles is a way to abbreviate the nations. In Romans 11 "Gentiles" means all other nations whom God loves and wants to bring into the commonwealth in the Age to Come. Paul can say to Gentile believers, "I speak to you, Gentiles," without any pejorative or negative prejudice. See Markus Bockmuehl, *Jewish Law in Gentile Churches* (Edinburg: T & T Clark, 2000). Bockmuehl brilliantly develops the theme of Jewish and Gentile distinction in the application of Torah.

[8]   Biblical unity is not the kind of unity that says, "Well, theology is unimportant; whatever you believe is fine. If you claim to speak in tongues, we're all together in unity. Well, I know you left your wife for your secretary, but let's not allow that to hurt our unity!"

I once heard someone who professed a desire for unity say, "Doctrine divides; Christ unites." What does that mean? Which Christ? As soon as you say the one who died and rose again, you've got doctrine. If we are not united by the foundational doctrines (teachings) of the Word of God, then we won't even know what we're talking about when we say the word *Messiah* or *Christ*.

The oneness that Yeshua prayed for comes through the work of eldership. Paul, in Ephesians 4:11–13, said that the fivefold ministry (apostles, prophets, pastors, evangelists, and teachers) will equip the saints for the work of the ministry until we all are unified in the faith (as in John 17) and the knowledge of the Son of God. Leadership is given to disciple, correct, and build people into community. Yeshua commanded the apostles to teach obedience to all that he commanded (Matt. 28:19, 20). A mature person is one who obeys Yeshua fully and part of this obedience is to seek the unity of all believers.

The body of believers is called to be the commonwealth of Israel, modeling the same kind of oneness among ourselves that the Messiah modeled between him and the Father. This will move those of Israel who do not yet believe in Yeshua to jealousy and will hasten the Second Coming of the Messiah, Yeshua.

2

The Early Church and the
Beginning of Decline

I look at the history of the Church as a repeated cycle of decline
and restoration. At present, I see so much church decline in this
country that I have to really be walking by faith in God's Word
and not by sight to believe in restoration. In many U.S. cities,
the Church is in a sad state. When the incidence of premarital
sexual relations is only slightly less among young believers
than the 73 percent in the secular world as a whole, we have
major problems.[1] We must raise our young people to walk in
purity, remaining uninfluenced by the world. Tragically, the
Church has become both ghettoized and compromised in her
relationship with the world. She is not *in* the world like she
is commanded to be, but she is *of* the world like she is commanded not to be—full of immorality and seeking mostly after
self-centered personal peace and affluence.

The Church before the fall of Jerusalem was not a perfect
church either. After the day of Pentecost, there was a brief
period of very high unity and power in the Church (Acts
2:42ff). The levels of carnality that needed to be overcome
are graphically described in the letters of Paul (see the Corin-
thian correspondence). The prayer of Yeshua in John 17 also
needed fulfillment in the first century, just like in our day.

---

[1]   These statistics vary somewhat but are generally available and annually revised
in the Barna Research Group website. See also The Buster Report: A New Generation
of Adults Discuss Their Life and Spirituality by David Kinnamon. Also on the Barna
website, www.barna.org.

However, there were several features of the Church before Jerusalem's fall that remain key aspects of the Church and that will fulfill Yeshua's prayer in John 17 and Paul's teaching in Ephesians 4.

First, there was a basic unity of the Church in every city. Whether a church of one hundred or of thousands, it was possible to address one church in every city. There was no competition among various denominations and streams in the body of believers. In the days of Revelation, there were meetings in different homes in each city.[2] Yet the Church was addressed as one church in each city. Contrary to writers today who warn against movements for Church unity (and there is a real danger from sloppy movements of unity in which right doctrine and behavior do not count for much), the apostles warn insistently against divisions and schisms.

Second, the Church before the fall of Jerusalem was in touch with its Jewish roots. The Jerusalem church had the respect and leadership of the Church as a whole. The apostles were Jewish. Therefore, a biblically rooted Jewish understanding of the meaning of Israel and the Church was normal. This will again be the case in the last days' Church (not the apostate church that will oppose the true Church). The last days' Church will be solidly based on apostolic doctrine, which will include a right understanding of the Jewishness of the Church.

Third, the first-century Church was familiar with the Holy Spirit's supernatural gifts. The Spirit's power was a normal experience in the life of the Church. Therefore, Paul only needed to write correctives about how the gifts of the Holy Spirit were to be expressed. The last days' Church will be strong in the use of the Holy Spirit's gifts.[3]

---

[2] Two books that give strong support for this statement are Robert Banks, *Paul's Idea of Community, the Early House Churches in Their Historical Setting* (Exeter: Paternoster Press, 1980) and Phillip Esler, *Modeling Early Christianity-Social-Scientific Studies on the N. T. Text in its Context* (New York: Rudledge, 1995).

[3] For the theological case of the continuation of the gifts after the first century and more, see Jack Deere, *Surprised by the Power of the Holy Spirit* (Grand Rapids: Zondervan, 1993), Appendix B, 229 ff.

Fourth, a plurality of elders governed the first-century Church, like the synagogue.[4] What is often known as *fivefold ministry* (apostles, prophets, evangelists, pastors, and teachers) was the leadership paradigm for the Church. In addition to fivefold ministry, we also see government by a mutually accountable eldership in each city and in every local congregational expression in the first-century Church.

In my view, the beginning of decline was the rejection of the Church's self-understanding with regard to Israel. Unlike some restoration teachers I have heard, I do not look at the decline as beginning with the loss of the Holy Spirit's gifts in the second century. I believe the supernatural gifts never disappeared completely although there was a decline in the use of these gifts.[5]

The Church Loses Its Jewish Roots

Before the loss of the Spirit's gifts, the gentile leaders in the Church exhibited a tragic rejection of their Jewish roots. I believe that this was the decline's real beginning. When Jerusalem fell, many Gentiles in the Church took this as Israel's final repudiation by God. The fall and destruction of Jerusalem was greatly significant to Israel and the Church. The evidence for church history between 70 C.E. and 90 C.E. is not clear. S. G. F. Brandon, a scholar with whom I do not agree in many respects, accurately calls the period of 70 to 90 C.E. the tunnel period of New Testament history.[6] We have so little informa-

---

[4]   Steven Cato, *Reconstructing the First Century Synagogue* (London: T & T Clark, 2007), 120, 136, 141,173.

[5]   The gifts are the graces of the Holy Spirit whereby the Holy Spirit is powerfully present. These graces are types of empowerment provided by God for what we are called to do. I think that if you study the meaning of the term Holy Spirit in first-century Judaism, you will find that where the Holy Spirit is present to a significant extent, there are outward manifestations of the Holy Spirit. Holy Spirit power and Holy Spirit manifestations were indistinguishable from one another in the first-century mind and were not easily separable. When you have one, you have the other. It is only in later Greek-influenced thinking that one tries to divide the two.

[6]   S. G. F. Brandon, *The Fall of Jerusalem and the Christian Church* (London: S.P.C.K., 1968).

tion until the early writings of the gentile Church fathers, in the second century. We do know that at the other end of that tunnel period was a great change in the Church's understanding of Israel.

At this point in history, all of the Jewish apostles were gone, and three great changes are discernible.

First, the destruction of Jerusalem and the scattering of many of the Jewish people were taken as showing God's ultimate and total rejection of Israel. Many church leaders were judging by sight instead of by the Word.

Second, a tremendous love and identification with Hellenistic culture was more prevalent. In the second century and even more so in the third, church fathers saw the writings of the Greek philosophers as almost equal to the Old Testament. Such Hellenistic writings were seen as preparatory revelation for the New Testament. The early church fathers highly esteemed the works of Plato, Aristotle, and other Greek thinkers. Greek culture was something they found difficult to transcend. There were, however, exceptions like Tertullian who famously stated, "What indeed has Athens to do with Jerusalem?"[7]

There were good and bad features of ancient Greek culture. The Greek language enabled precise definition and coherent presentations of truth, which were very important in fostering a more universal understanding and, by extension, international unity. It was a great advantage and perhaps one of the reasons God chose the Greek language and culture as a vessel to spread the Gospel. Rules of logic and rhetoric are important aspects of Paul's presentation.

However, there were negative elements in Hellenistic culture as well. In saying this, I am not advocating some ideas about Hellenism, for example, embracing Sunday as a day of rest and worship, Supposed roots and parallels in paganism are irrelevant as long as explicit pagan practices are rejected. One negative result was not respecting the biblical calendar's

---

[7]   Tertullian, *Heretics*, 7; Ante-Nicean Fathers, vol. 3 (New York: Cosimo Classics, 2007), 246.

importance, which caused the first century Messianic Jews to begin separating from their own Jewish communities.

The real problem with Hellenistic thinking is subtler and deeper. Greek Platonic philosophy held that the realm of abstraction, the idea that the abstract is the "really real" and is more important is contrary to biblical understanding. God is timeless, and saved souls live in a timeless existence. Once this is embraced, the concrete salvation of this world is downplayed or even denied. Hence, the millennium seemed unspiritual to some of the early church fathers. Once God is defined as timeless and passive, the higher truth shown in the Bible's anthropomorphic metaphors are explained away. However, such metaphors are the best way to understand God as one who is involved with us, who loves, who is angry, and who responds to prayer. That really changes history.

Hellenistic thought also diminishes our view of the Kingdom in all of its real and current worldly dimensions. Salvation as escape is not the Jewish biblical emphasis. The Church embraced the doctrine of the resurrection of the body, but Greek-influenced theologians struggled with this doctrine and sometimes placed the emphasis on the soul's immortality.

Third, responses of the early Church to severe persecution at the end of the first century and in the early second often alienated the Church from Israel. We must appreciate the heroism of believers in those early days. Many died as martyrs; some were fed to the lions. However, some Christians wanted to deny their connection to the Jewish people because at first the Romans understood Christians to be a sect of Judaism. After the first revolt against Rome, the Jewish people were not a favored people in the Roman Empire. Josephus's writings sought to remedy this situation. After they revolted again under Shimon bar Kokhba in the 130s, the Jewish people were even more despised.

After the first revolt, there was still a significant Jewish population in the land of Israel. Before this, Judaism had been given the status of a legitimate religion in the Roman Empire, giving them a special legal privilege to not have to bow in worship to the emperor and the idols of Rome. The Jews were the only exception. In the beginning, the Christians almost wanted to be seen as Jews so that they were part of a legitimate religion and not persecuted. However, after Israel lost its favor with Rome, to be identified with something Jewish was to open oneself to more persecution.[8] This made it expedient for gentile believers to identify themselves as good Roman citizens and Greek-cultured people rather than to connect with Jewish roots.

The Roman emperor in the 90s adopted the seven-day week of the Jewish people. Sunday, the Day of the Sun, was chosen and became a part of Roman pagan religious observance. The other days of the week were named after Roman gods.[9] The Church generally accepted Sunday as its day of worship[10] and other groups eventually adapted the same practice. For example, the German version is Monday—Lunar day, Tuesday—Mercury day, Wednesday—Woden's day, and Thursday—Thor's day.[11] The Church identified the theme of light in regard to the sun with the light of the Son, Yeshua. Therefore, the Church chose Sunday as a day given to the Lord. Although Sunday had been readily provided by the empire, the Church gave biblical meaning to the day. This can be seen in the writings of the church fathers in the second century.[12] As time progressed the emphasis on Sunday as the day to celebrate the resurrection of Yeshua became more pronounced. This was quite natural since Yeshua's resurrection took place

[8]   Magnus Zitterholm, *The Formation of Christianity in Antioch* (New Albany: Routledge, 2006). His book is an important resource not only for Antioch, but as a model for other cities.

[9]   Samuele Bacchochi, *From Sabbath to Sunday* (Appleton: The Pontifical Georgian University Press, 1977). I disagree with his understanding on Sabbath requirements for Gentiles because the Sabbath is part of a covenant with the Jewish people in the Ten Words Covenant (Exod. 20). Rabbinic Judaism understood that not all of the ten were for Gentiles. Yet I think his understanding of the progression of change is excellent. *The Catholic Encyclopedia*, vol. 3 (New York: Encyclopedia Press, 1908), 158, 168. The last reference notes that Sunday worship was not mentioned until Justin.

[10]   I believe the Resurrection occurred on the first day of the week. I know some argue in the Messianic Movement that it occurred on Shabbat, but I think the logical conclusion from Scripture is to rest on the seventh day. The first day is creation, the Feast of First Fruits, and the Feast of Resurrection.

[11]   Ibid., pp. 158–168, also see website, www.Exhibits.Org/calendars/week.

[12]   See Bacciochi for the full account.

on the first day of the week. (However, there is no evidence that God intended to change the Sabbath day. This denial of the Sabbath's legitimacy for Jews, including Messianic Jews, was wrong. The seventh-day Sabbath was not given to gentile believers as a covenant responsibility.)

The Denial of the Saved Remnant

The statement of Justin Martyr typifies the growing consensus that rejected the legitimacy of the saved remnant of Israel's identity. Reflecting this in a later century, Jerome famously said, "He who will be both Christian and Jew can be neither Christian nor Jew."[13] The saved remnant of Israel has a role both as part of the nation of Israel and as the Jewish part of the universal body of believers. This is a very important theological concept. Justin's denial of the legitimacy of Jewish life in Jesus was part of his denial of the continued role and future for nationalized Israel. This early rejection of the saved remnant planted the seed for Jewish persecution by churches in later centuries, coming to fullness in the Holocaust.

Many in the Christian community throughout the centuries have denied the saved remnant of Israel and identified with Greco-Roman roots instead of Jewish roots. Instead of encouraging the growth of the saved remnant of Israel, to which the rest of the body is joined, the Church has often encouraged their isolation and decline. Parallel to the Christian community, the Jewish community also rejected the saved remnant of Israel as a legitimate part of Israel. Jewish leaders claimed that Yeshua-believing Jews followed a false Messiah and were traitors because they did not fight under bar Kokhba, whom Rabbi Akiba declared the Messiah in the 130s.[14] The saved remnant of Israel declined to a small number by the end of the second

---

[13] See Daniel Boyarin, *Borderlines* (Philadelphia: University of Pennsylvania Press, 2004), 207. Isadorous Hilburg, ed., "Corpus Scripturum Eccleasticoram Latinorum,, Jerome. Correspondence," Verlog der Osterreichishen Academie der Wuschaften 55, (1996): 381–383.

[14] "Bar Kokhba," *Encyclopedia Judaica* vol. B (1972): 230. See Jerusalem Talmud, Talan, 4:8.

century and shrank to an almost nonexistence by the fifth century.[15] Probably Islam's seventh-century onslaught wiped out the last of the saved remnant of Israel as a corporate body. It may be that believing Jews were forcibly converted to Islam.

I am not arguing for becoming anti-Hellenistic. However, the value of Hellenistic understanding should never have superseded Jewish roots of understanding. The sad history recounted here is a short summary of complex developments that established error in the Church. The Church was not wrong to contextualize the Gospel but was wrong to not respect the Jewish people and especially the saved remnant of the Jewish people.

[15]   Ray Pritz, *Nazarean Jewish Christianity: From the End of the New Testament Period Until Its Disappearance in the Fourth Century* (Jerusalem: Magnus Press, 1992). B. Bagatti, *The Church from the Circumcision* (Rome: Pontifical Biblical Institute, 1971).

3

Rome's Elevation and the Decline of the Church's Jewish Identity

Consequences for the Church for Rejecting Her Jewish Roots

What happens when the Church denies its Jewish roots? The Church can no longer understand theology with accuracy. The Bible says in Romans 3:1, "What advantage is there in being a Jew? Much in every way, they are given the very words of God." Two of the gifts given to the Jewish people are revelation and interpretation of God's Word. There were many declines that took place in the third century, perhaps as a result of this repudiation of Jewish believers.

Even though the Holy Spirit was still at work and great insight was gained, other developments were negative. One of these changes was in the area of Church government. The apostles, I believe, understood congregational government as vested in elder plurality as in the synagogue. The term *elder* was the same word used to refer to the elders of the gate in ancient Israel. During the early years of Israel's nationhood, judges always functioned in the context of plurality; however, among this plurality, specific judges rose to prominence to lead the other judges. It was natural.

The plurality of elders in the first-century synagogue was parallel to the government structure of the plurality of judges in ancient Israel's cities. The Church, however, was looking to Greco-Roman models for its self-understanding. Not only were its theological concepts defined in Greek terms rather than Jewish terms, but the Church understood its government in Roman terms. It patterned its government structure and hierarchy after the Roman models of civil government. The functions of the Church's government officials were parallel in authority and extent to those in the Roman government. The pope paralleled the emperor and Rome and was defined as the most prominent bishopric.

The term *pontiff* is derived from Roman government. It was originally a term referring to the Roman emperor. The Church saw the pope as the leader of all kings and thus used the term to designate the pope. The bishop became parallel to the ruler of a city in the empire. Where was Israel in all this? Where were the Jewish models? It would seem the Church's theology and practice was declining from Jewish origins to Roman secular customs.

Parallel to this decline is the loss of the Holy Spirit's gifts. A theology later developed to affirm this loss as though God intended the gifts to cease. Augustine, in the fifth century, codified both declines as improvement or progression. Augustine taught that there was no future for the Jewish people but that they were preserved to be an example of what happens to a people who reject God. Augustine said that they would never again enter their land and they would never again enter God's favor because they crucified the Messiah-God.[1] Augustine also explained that the Spirit's gifts were only intended for the purpose of testifying to the apostolic leaders' authority of the first century. (Augustine later experienced genuine gifts of the Spirit and changed his view.[2] Protestant theology followed Augustine's earlier views on the gifts.)

[1] James Parkes, *The Conflict of the Church and the Synagogue* (New York: Atheneum, 1969). Daniel Juster, *Jewish Roots* (Shippensburg: Destiny Image, 1995), 143.
[2] Augustine in his later life discovered real miracles and gifts and then changed on this point as noted in Jack Deere, *Surprised by the Power of the Holy Spirit* (Grand Rapids: Zondervan, 1993), Appendix B.

The Work of God in the Patristic Church

It is important that in giving such a simple summary we avoid an error to think that the Spirit of God was not working in the Church because of the specific declines we have mentioned. It is not as though all aspects of the Church were in decline. Indeed, progress was made in some fronts while decline was seen on other fronts. The Church produced amazing and godly leaders, such as Clement, Iraneaus, Tertullian, and Augustine. We need to avoid the error of thinking that despite an overemphasis on Greek thinking, all of the Church's conceptualizing was wrong.

In addition, we need to recognize that Greek modes of thinking provide helpful perspectives as well, as long as the original Hebraic context is kept in mind as foundational. This is true for many languages, but we must especially ask why God saw fit to give the New Covenant revelation in the Greek language. Not only was Greek a more universal language, but it was a language with a great ability to express many facets of truth with great precision.

The patristic leaders (early church fathers) faced many challenges. A great variety of views battled for acceptance among Christians. This included Eastern religious influences through a religious orientation called gnosticism.[3] To battle these tendencies, the Church gathered its leaders to define its faith against those foreign influences. In an effort to safeguard the Church, it enhanced the office of the bishop.

It appears that at first the presbytery (or council) of elders governed the Church of Jerusalem. There was a leadership succession as elders ordained elders reaching back to the

---

[3] Gnosticism is an ancient heretical religious belief system that emphasized a strong distinction between the material and spiritual world. They believed that humans were confined to the material world and were unable to ascend into the spirit's superior world without special revelation (gnosis). Secret knowledge marked Gnosticism as the only hope for people to be freed from the confines of the material world. As such, Christian leaders strongly opposed Gnosticism because it affirmed a salvation rooted in a "hidden knowledge" rather than in the person and work of Yeshua.

apostles. It is natural in any plural group of leaders that someone emerges with greater leadership gifts. Such a person leads the presbytery. The use of the word *bishop* changed from its New Testament origin as a synonym for elders and was now reserved for the leader of the city's presbytery. He was considered to be in succession to the apostles and to have attained the apostolic office.

Bishops ordained new bishops. The bishops followed the Roman models of the city's government. With this authority, the bishops became the key leaders in safeguarding scriptural truth. It appears from the writings of the ante-Nicene fathers that the bishop was originally the first among equals in the council (similar to the city elders who made decisions in a plurality).[4]

By the end of the second century, the bishop functioned as the decision-making head, the "monarchical bishop" as he came to be known. Although Victor of Rome, at the end of the second century, asserted his governmental supremacy over all other bishops, the eastern bishops did not accept this and from then until now still maintain a greater plurality among the college of bishops.[5]

Councils of bishops defined our basic doctrines of the nature of God, the nature of Yeshua as fully human and fully divine, and other aspects of doctrine. Although Messianic Jews saw these conceptions as overly Greek, I believe that the Spirit of God worked in spite of a lack of appreciation for Jewish roots.[6] Nicea in 325 C.E. defined the triune nature of God as one God eternally existent in three persons, equal in essence as divinity but not identical in function. Chalcedon clarified the conception of Yeshua as one person with both a divine and human nature. After his incarnation, the pre-existent divine Messiah became fully human and fully divine.

---

[4]   This is my own conclusion from reading the *Ante-Nicean Fathers*. See also, Mark Mattison, *The Rise of the Clergy* (Dearing: Grace Ministries Publications, 2007). See also, J. N. D. Kelly, *Early Christian Doctrines* (New York: Harper, 1978), 3–28.
[5]   "Easter Dating," *The New Catholic Encyclopedia*, vol. O. (New York: Catholic University of America and McGraw Hill, 2002), 796.

The Church basically got this right. It was probably the best possible statement in the Greek language. Unifying the Church in basic doctrine was no small task. Evangelical Christians to this day affirm the understanding of Nicea and Chalcedon. These statements of doctrine were put in creedal forms and recited by many in historic denominations. The Church did compromise with Greek philosophy. Its concepts of God's timelessness, impassability, and changelessness, not just in character but in all senses, showed such wrong Greek influences. Nevertheless, it did repel the dangerous errors of gnosticism and paganism. The Church was not perfect in this by any means, but it was largely successful.

It is important to note the role of Constantine. After his profession of the Christian faith, Constantine made Christianity a legal religion in Rome. Christianity had become so widespread that Constantine saw it as a possible means to unify his empire.[7] Toward this end, Constantine gave himself to foster the First Council of Nicea.

Two errors in interpreting this council are common among Messianic Jews. One is that the decisions of this council are explicitly anti-Jewish and anti-Messianic Jewish. This is not true. Not one canon or doctrinal position was explicitly anti-Jewish. Some point to the separate letter written by Constantine as proving that antisemitism was really behind these decisions. Even if Constantine was hostile toward Jews, this bias does not gain expression in the canons.

Instead of antisemitism, we should note that there were other concerns behind these decisions–like the decision made concerning the celebration of Easter. There was a strong desire

---

[6]   Oscar Skarsaune of the Free Lutheran Theological faculty in Norway has written extensively on this. He is an expert in early Jewish Christianity and patristics. His argument is very forceful that the conceptions of Nicea and Chalcedon were basically correct if the Greek language was to be used. His book *Incarnation, Myth, or Fact* is a key book on this subject.

[7]   "Easter Dating," *The New Catholic Encyclopedia*, vol. C, (New York: Catholic University of America and McGraw Hill, 2002), 228, 299. The writer notes that this is the inference from the writings of Eusebius, *Eccleseastical History* and *Life of Constantine* and Constantine's Letter to the Bishops at Arles.

to be the most accurate concerning the actual day of the resurrection. This entailed solving complex issues of solar and lunar time and keeping the right reconciliation between them. In all probability those who think that Nicea included explicit anti-Jewish canons have confused it with Nicea II. This second ecumenical Council of Nicea in 787 C.E. included explicit canons condemning anyone who professed faith in Yeshua and who maintains Jewish tradition.[8] This was in line with previous regional councils that included anti-Jewish canons. Some canons explicitly rejected Jewish life in Yeshua. Examples of such councils are Alvira, Spain, in 307 C.E. and Antioch in 316 C.E.[9]

The second error is to think that Nicea created Church doctrine on the deity of Yeshua and the Trinity. However, even a cursory reading of the *Ante-Nicene Fathers* shows beyond a reasonable doubt that a basic consensus on those doctrines had already taken root in the Church. Nicea's decisions in this regard were not novel.

We have often read that Jewish bishops were intentionally left out of the Council of Nicea due to the lack of Jewish names on the list of the bishops. However, we are not aware of any practicing Messianic Jewish bishops by the time of Nicea. There is no record of their explicit exclusion although this is possible.

---

[8]   "Since some of those who come from the *religion of the Hebrews* mistakenly think to make a mockery of Christ who is God, *pretending to become Christians*, but denying Christ in private by both secretly continuing to observe the Sabbath and maintaining other Jewish practices, we decree that they *shall not be received to communion or at prayer or into the church*, but rather let them openly be Hebrews according to their own religion; *they should not baptize their children or buy, or enter into possession of, a slave.* But if one of them makes his conversion with a sincere faith and heart, and pronounces his confession wholeheartedly, disclosing their practices and objects in the hope that others may be refuted and corrected, such a person should be welcomed and baptized along with his children, and care should be taken that they abandon Hebrew practices. However if they are not of this sort, they should certainly not be welcomed." From Norman Tanner, *Decrees of the Ecumenical Councils* (Lanham: Shed and Ward, 1990), 787 (emphasis mine).
[9]   From research done by the author and Fr. Peter Hocken at Catholic University in original Latin and translated. Available from the Toward Jerusalem Council II, 6304 Beltline Road, Dallas, Texas.

Reaching back to the end of the second century, it is worthwhile to note that the Eastern Church at that time was very oriented to the Jewish calendar and kept the lunar calendar to mark the death and resurrection of Yeshua, celebrating them together on the fourteenth of Nisan.[10] The debate between Pope Victor and Polycrates of Antioch, each condemning the practice of the other, is of note. Victor sought to enforce a Sunday celebration of the Resurrection. The celebration of First Fruits on the first day of the week harkened back to the Temple–sadducean calandar in contradistinction to the pharisaic–rabbinic calendar. In some years the Church's celebration of First Fruits was the same day as the Church's celebration of the Resurrection. Polycrates defended an older Eastern Church practice of celebrating the death and Resurrection on the fourteenth and fifteenth of Nisan, irrespective of the day of the week. Both

---

[10] See "Quartodaiceman Controversy," *New Catholic Encyclopedia* vol. Q (New York: Catholic University of America and McGraw Hill, Year), 8, 9. Quote included here from Polycrates:

"We observe the exact day; neither adding, nor taking away. For in Asia also great lights have fallen asleep, which shall rise again on the day of the Lord's coming, when he shall come with glory from heaven, and shall seek out all the saints. Among these are Philip, one of the twelve apostles, who fell asleep in Hierapolis; and his two aged virgin daughters, and another daughter, who lived in the Holy Spirit and now rests at Ephesus; and, moreover, *John*, who was both a witness and a teacher, who reclined upon the bosom of the Lord, and, being a priest, wore the sacerdotal plate. He fell asleep at Ephesus. And *Polycarp* in Smyrna, who was a bishop and martyr; and *Thraseas*, bishop and martyr from Eumenia, who fell asleep in Smyrna. Why need I mention the bishop and martyr *Sagaris* who fell asleep in Laodicea, or the blessed *Papirius*, or *Melito*, the Eunuch who lived altogether in the Holy Spirit, and who lies in Sardis, awaiting the episcopate from heaven, when he shall rise from the dead? All these observed the *fourteenth day of the passover* according to the Gospel, deviating in no respect, but following the rule of faith. And I also, Polycrates, the least of you all, do according to the tradition of my relatives, some of whom I have closely followed. For seven of my relatives were bishops; and I am the eighth. And my relatives always observed the day when the people put away the leaven. I, therefore, brethren, who have lived sixty-five years in the Lord, and have met with the brethren throughout the world, and have gone through every Holy Scripture, am not affrighted by terrifying words. For those greater than I have said, 'We ought to obey God rather than man' … I could mention the bishops who were present, whom I summoned at your desire; whose names, should I write them, would constitute a great multitude. And they, beholding my littleness, gave their consent to the letter, knowing that I did not bear my gray hairs in vain, but had always governed my life by the Lord Jesus" (Eusebius, *Church History*. Book V, Chapter 24).

the East and the West claimed the basis for their argument in ancient tradition going back to the apostles. Nicea did finally bring unity on this issue to East and West. We do see a sad departure from some aspects of Jewish roots in this debate. Over a half-century later, Justinian I made Christianity the state religion. Eventually the old Roman pagan religions were made illegal. The marriage of Church and state brought tremendous problems. The state used the Church to extend its power, and the Church used the state and the power of the sword to foster its doctrinal orthodoxy. More than three hundred years of Christian witness, during which Christians gave up their lives before the sword but never used the sword to extend the Kingdom of God came to an end. The great orthodox Jewish philosopher Eliezer Berkowitz notes that no persecution of the Jews came from free churches, only from the combination of Church and state power.[11]

Two other developments should be stressed. One was the loss of the house as the basic gathering place of believers. Though larger church gatherings preceded Constantine and church buildings did exist, the periodically persecuted Church mostly met in homes.[12] This provided intimacy and accountability. First Corinthians 12 and 14 show us a meeting structure that is only possible in a smaller gathering.

Constantine embarked upon a great building program, and the idea of the Church as a place for the priesthood to dispense benefits to the laity became more firmly rooted. Larger gatherings of celebration are not wrong, but the loss of the house group as the basic gathering spot was tragic. Ministering to one another through the Holy Spirit is a sacramental part of our spiritual life grounded in biblical teaching.

---

[11]   Eliezer Berkowitz, *Faith after the Holocaust* (New York: KTAV, 1973).
[12]   Bruce Wardell, *A Short History of Church Building* (www.brucewardell.com, 2004).
   Note that in 323, Constantine subsidized church building with government money. In 324 he wrote to the bishops to be active in building church buildings. Also in Eusebius, *Life of Constantine*.

The second development is a source of great wonder. The Church upheld the sanctity of the Hebrew Scriptures against the attacks of the Marcionites. The idea that the Church totally rejected the Hebrew Scriptures and fully lost its Jewish roots is false. The loss of Jewish roots was only partial. The way that the Church did appropriate Jewish roots is amazing. Although the Church claimed that the New Covenant had replaced Moses, it did not follow Marcion and reject the Hebrew Scriptures entirely. Although speaking against Jewish biblical practices for both Jews and Gentiles certainly looked like the rejection of the Hebrew Bible, the reality is much more complex. The Church understood that the Hebrew Scriptures provided universal moral teaching. Hence, much of the Church's moral teaching was based in the same Hebrew Scriptures that the New Covenant transcended.

In addition, the Church sought to appropriate some of the very Temple rituals described in the Hebrew Bible and give it a New Covenant reapplication. This began quite early. The celebration of the Lord's Supper (Eucharist) was practiced as a fulfilled form of Temple sacrifice. Language for these meanings begins with the New Covenant Scriptures. In the second century officiants acting as priests mediated the elements of the Lord's Supper as a fellowship offering eaten by worshippers.

When Constantine's church building program flourished, the idea of that building as a temple became widespread. In 1 Corinthians 3:16, the corporate congregation, not the building, is said to be the temple of the Holy Spirit. The layout of the new temple had a Most Holy Place with a screen blocking this place where only the officiating priest(s) could enter. It contained an altar where the bread and wine (the sacrificial elements) were placed. The later development of a choir behind the altar was based on the Levitical system of Israel. The congregation was in the courtyard. The narthex was the outer court. Parallels to the Temple also included an eternal light, the seven-branched menorah, the altar, the use of incense, and the laver for washing (only later used for baptism). The priests and bishops wore special liturgical garments as in the ancient

Temple. (Something of these elements are preserved in most Protestant churches, including liturgical garments, the altar where the elements of the Lord's Supper are placed, the menorah, the eternal light, and more.)

The extent of this development is, of course, not in the Bible. Yet in some ways this does powerfully portray biblical meanings and fulfillment. Nonetheless, disturbingly the Church became the place for dispensing a product: the sacrament first of all and then a homily. This replaced the house congregation, which is a great loss, though one can appreciate the Temple-like service as a supplement.

It is important as well to understand something of the liturgy's development that also had Hebrew scriptural patterns to inspire it. Liturgy is basically the work of the people in prayer and worship, but the word takes on the meaning of worship that is authorized and repeated. As in the ancient Temple, the Church was concerned to cover the most important basics. Fixed liturgies were great teaching tools for the people. As preserved in Catholic, Eastern Orthodox, Lutheran, and Anglican churches, there is an amazing and deep expression of biblical truth. This is also true of the old hymns and odes. However, the Protestant temple, except among Anglicans and Lutherans, significantly reduced adhering to church liturgy.

There is a lesson in this for charismatic independent churches in our time. The elevation of the meaning of Yeshua's death and Resurrection, the confession of our beliefs in the creed, the worship, and reverence upon receiving the bread and wine of the Lord's Supper should give some charismatic independent churches pause. This would produce amazing and glorious church music traditions with musically sung poetry. We see the heights of this in the Lutheran work of Johann Sebastian Bach.

In so many ways I wonder at this mixture of very good and very bad in the Church's development. The good is seen in the reverence for God's salvation in Yeshua, the Eucharist, and the Torah's application for moral teaching. The bad was in the defense of a state–church doctrine enforcement by the sword and the abstract ideas of God from Greek philsophy.

In addition, rejecting the positive destiny of the Jewish people was a major failure.

Jewish Roots and Spiritual Power

The church fathers' rejection of the Jewish people was connected to the teaching that by calling for Yeshua's crucifixion, the Jewish people as a whole came under a most terrible curse of God. I do not believe that this is the emphasis of the New Covenant Scriptures; rather, I believe that the full responsiblity for rejecting Yeshua came after the apostles' testimony of the Resurrection of Yeshua. The testimony's full meaning was that Israel had been visited in a special way. The failure to embrace this apostolic witness led to the fullfillment of Yeshua's prophecy that Jerusalem would be destroyed. Because Jerusalem's leadership had a representative role, I believe that history shows that the Jewish people have not had the full protection of God as promised in the Torah.

Israel's preservation and scattering, even in persecution, shows God's covenant faithfulness. Augustine is a powerful patristic voice in rejecting Israel's continued covenant status with God. Divine preservation of the Jewish people was only to show what happens to a people who reject God's revelation. In his earlier writings, Augustine also interpreted the absence of the Holy Spirit's gifts as a sign that they were only for the purpose of establishing the early Church.[13] This became the standard Protestant view.

Many other Catholic and Eastern Orthodox teachers limited supernatural gifts and miracles to special saints. The power of the signs, wonders, and manifestations of the Kingdom in the New Testament become reinterpreted in a way to discount their importance with the following kinds of statements: "These

---

[13]   Other people develop their theology to defend their experience. They want to feel okay and that where they are in life is fine, so they rationalize their beliefs through a well-developed theology. Augustine was a very great man of God in many ways. However, when he saw the Church's powerlessness and political power replacing real spiritual power, he theologized it as the way God intended it to be.

things happened so that the apostles' authority would be accepted," "These things were only needed before the Scriptures were written," "These things were attestations of Yeshua's divinity and have nothing to do with our being filled with the Spirit," or "Experiencing the Spirit in this way was only for the special saints." Were the miracles, signs, and wonders really attestations to Yeshua's divinity or were they more attestations of his being filled with the power of the Spirit? I believe Scriptures' testimony is that Yeshua did not draw from his own divinity. He could have. He could have called for the twelve legions of angels and avoided the cross. But to be the perfect example for us, he lived as a human being filled with the power of the Holy Spirit. In him we see the potential of a man filled with the Holy Spirit. We will never fully attain his perfection and power, but we can reach our potential in him and be more like him.

The doctrine of *cessationism* (the idea that some gifts of the Holy Spirit ceased after the apostolic period) is related to a rejection of the Jewish understanding of the Holy Spirit. The Jewish understanding of the Holy Spirit is clearly found in Jewish sources and is also a central aspect of understanding Christianity's biblically Jewish roots. This is well documented in W. D. Davie's classic *Paul and Rabbinic Judaism*. In first-century Judaism, where the Spirit was present to any great degree, prophecy, signs, and wonders were a corollary.

All this is not to say that Christianity alone was influenced by Hellenism. Judaism had its own Greek influence upon it. One can see significant Greek influence in the Talmud. I believe that Yeshua's battle with the religious leaders was in part a battle with Hellenism in Judaism. Hellenism turned Judaism toward a rationalistic orientation. We cannot underestimate the influence of the Hellenistic world on both Judaism and Christianity.[14]

---

[14] The Hellenistic world is not all bad. There are certain dimensions of truth from Noah and from natural revelation that are found in Hellenistic culture. But there is a lot that is not good. Hellenistic–Roman culture affected most people during that particular time in history.

The Church of the Dark and Middle Ages

The Church did continue to advance during the Middle Ages. Pious missionaries who truly loved the Lord spread the Gospel to many lands. Patrick of Ireland was typical of the best. With signs and wonders, he established the Church in that land. The Church also made doctrinal progress. For example, in the twelfth century, St. Anselm first put forth the theology of Yeshua's death as a substitutionary satisfaction for our sins. His view became the standard Catholic view through Thomas Aquinas and the standard Protestant understanding through the Reformers in the sixteenth century. This is the primary view of Yeshua's atonement among evangelical Christians even in our own day.

In spite of the good during this period, another development contrary to Jewish roots took root in the early Middle Ages. A foundational Jewish ethic was that all Jewish men are responsible before God and, therefore, should be able to read the synagogue scrolls for themselves. They needed to be able to teach God's Word to their children. Jewish men were expected to know how to read and write to accomplish this. In the Church because of the hierarchy, the laity could become illiterate. Much emphasis was placed on the Church's teaching ministry and the people were expected to follow their leaders. They were to believe what they were told without questioning authority.

Teaching leadership is certainly important in the Church. However, this does not replace the importance of an educated people as a check on false teaching. The knowledge of God's Word was therefore lost along with the very ideal of an educated people knowing the Word.[15] The Church abandoned the Jewish-rooted understanding that if God gave us the Torah and the Torah is the foundation of revelation, then everyone

---

[15]   The authority of leadership is to help to us in our understanding and interpretation of the Word. The check on that authority is that we are to read the Word to make sure our leaders are not erring on doctrine. However, when the masses are not allowed to know the Bible for themselves, then a very important safety net is removed.

needs to know the Torah. Historical evidence strongly suggests that most Jewish young men at the time of Yeshua understood and memorized the whole Torah, the Psalms, and many parts of the Prophets.

After Rome fell, some say the Dark Ages came. This is a gross oversimplification, but it is true there was a significant loss of learning. The loss of the knowledge of God's Word facilitated the acceptance of false doctrines. "Works" were joined to justification as being necessary for salvation instead of works done in faith as the fruit of justification.[16] It is only by unmerited grace that people are able to first believe and receive Yeshua as Lord and Savior into their lives. The idea of works, indulgences (purchasing the release of loved ones from purgatory), and all of the philosophies identified as part of Catholicism's decline are connected to the loss of the Word of God. Hierarchy, the ignorance of the masses, and forced conversions drove people away—the decline was massive. There is a decline when people who claim to be Christians hold forth their swords and say, "Believe and be baptized!" There is a decline when you believe that there is a purgatory from which people escape by friends and relatives purchasing their release. There is a decline when many priests cannot even read. There is a decline when higher clergy live in sumptuous luxury.

Cardinal Thomas Wolsey, at the beginning of the sixteenth century, had a bigger palace than King Henry VIII did. His life was in danger because King Henry was jealous, and so Cardinal Wolsey donated his palace to Henry. (There is nothing new under the sun. Today, some wealthy ministers in the Church think, *Well, I have a big ministry. Overseeing a big ministry is a similar responsibility to being a corporate executive, so I should live like the president of General Motors.* This is not new

---

[16]   Works should never be seen as ways to gain God's favor. We are saved only by faith through grace. Grace is the enabling power of obedience. Yet, I do not want to go to the other extreme, which teaches that we can be saved and continue to live in sin. Grace is always the empowerment of the Holy Spirit to obey.

thinking!) What was Cardinal Wolsey thinking? *I am head of the Roman Catholic Church of England. The Church is even more important and glorious than the civil state, so I should live at least as well as King Henry VIII.* The late Jamie Buckingham put it this way, "At a certain point we lose touch with reality."[17]

Were there any real believers during medieval Catholicism? Yes, there were many great examples. There were movements to purify the Church. Some monastic movements restored truths. Although the mass of Christians was not discipled, monasteries were places of discipleship. Consider St. Francis of Assisi, a great and godly man. In spite of all and contrary to the spirit of his age, St. Francis showed kindness to Jewish people.

Although there were true believers, still medieval Catholicism's developments are troubling. The doctrine of Mary and the saints as it is understood in the Catholic Church began at this time. The degree of authority attributed to the Pope and other doctrines expanded as well. (Vatican II restored a greater level of biblical truth to the Catholic Church while preserving some of these troubling doctrines.)

Another example of decline in this period was in the lack of purity in believers' lives. Priests and congregants alike were steeped in immorality, yet they were paying indulgences to get people out of purgatory. The Church was full of superstition, too. When you convert masses by the sword, their paganism remains part of their identity. Magic and paganism were still maintained in the European tribes after the state conquered these various peoples and imposed Christian doctrine and practice on them. Things got very dark. One of the superstitions was that relics, holy bones or objects, could provide healing. (Mark Twain remarked that there were

---

[17] I do believe in biblical prosperity but not opulence. I feel quite prosperous; I am not against prosperity. I do not believe I should come here in shredded garments and a hair shirt, which is the other aberration—asceticism. Asceticism is the pummeling of the body, embodying the stigmata, and living in poverty as a sign of piety. This is an unhealthy extreme, too.

enough relics of the cross sufficient to build the ark of Noah.) The Bible does teach that physical objects can carry spiritual power; however, the Church's emphasis on this was all out of biblical proportion.

This decline began with the rejection of Jewish roots. We always have a decline when we fail to honor our fathers and mothers. Even parents who may be terrible have at least preserved the life of their child. Without them the child would not have existed. Even in the worst family situation, there is something for which the child can thank God. There is always something for which we can honor our parents.[18]

The honoring of parents is a corporate principle as well. Israel is the parent of the Church, though a wayward one who did not submit to God. The saved remnant did submit to the righteousness of Yeshua. The Church is also a very wayward child. The Church's response to Israel has been very similar to the proud child who accepts the Lord but is arrogant against his unbelieving parents. By the same token, the charismatic movement, in being arrogant toward denominations, has become anarchistic and chaotic, even though the historic denominations gave birth to Christian religion as it is known today. I am not committed to the necessity of traditional denominations, but if new forms develop, they must learn from the lessons and wisdom of the past.

The decline also indicated an elevated degree of animosity toward the Jewish people. This book does not catalogue in detail the antisemitic actions of Christian leaders and people in Church history. The catalog is all too familiar. From the early centuries we have the terrible diatribe of St. Ambrose, who vilified the emperor's plans to rebuild a synagogue after antisemites destroyed it. We have the vile sermons against the Jews by John Chrysostom in the fifth century. Then came the local

---

[18] If you fail to honor your parents, instead of receiving the good from them and having an accurate understanding of the bad, you will repeat in your own life the wrong patterns through the sin of bitterness.

church councils that included language that demeaned Jews and demanded that Christians not have them bless their fields. There was the first expulsion of Jews from Spain in the seventh century. Then came the forced debates in the Middle Ages. The Jews were always proclaimed the losers. The expulsion from Spain under King Ferdinand and Queen Isabella, very pious Catholic leaders, in 1492 destroyed the greatest Jewish community of the Diaspora. Many Jews professed Christianity to stay but secretly practiced Jewish traditions. For this "terrible sin," the Inquisition was instituted. Those burned at the stake were in some ways like Messianic Jews, professing to believe in Yeshua but keeping Jewish life. We do not know how many actually believed in Yeshua or only said so to save their lives. This antisemitism was rooted in the early second-century Church. Would the Protestant Reformation readopt Jewish roots?

4

The Reformation

Into this darkness came the Reformation. When evil comes in like a flood, the Lord promises that he will raise up a standard (Is. 59:19 KJV). The Lord was never without a witness. There were the pre-Reformers, John Huss and John Wycliffe, as well as pious believers in the Catholic Church who remained faithful. Yet things became so dark that it is hard today to imagine just how bad it was. By the Reformation, there was a loss in understanding of biblical Jewish roots, biblical unity, fivefold ministry, government by a elder plurality locally and in each city, the Holy Spirit's gifts given to ordinary people, the ultimate place of scriptural authority, and justification by faith.

Reformation Under Luther

During this time a young priest in the Catholic Church was wrestling with the anxiety in his heart; his name was Martin Luther. He could not get peace with God through the disciplines including asceticism. Catholic doctrine was not working for him.[1] In his reading of Romans, he came to a new place of illumination. It was a conversion-like experience. He began to understand the Bible from a whole new perspective.

Luther did something at the risk of his life; he nailed ninety-five theses on the Wittenberg Church door. Luther's

---

[1] I am not anti-Catholic. There are saved Catholics, and today many Catholics embrace some of Martin Luther's corrections. By the same token, please do not think I am saying we should go back to the Catholic Church and that all is well with her today.

realization of those ninety-five theses only were the revelation of the Holy Spirit. They were a clear, passionate, and accurate statement of biblical truths long neglected and widely held by evangelical Christians today. That he could come to that understanding in the darkness of the times is amazing. That he took the courageous step to nail it on the door of the church to seek to bring reformation to the Catholic Church is even more astounding.

Luther did not want to leave the Catholic Church, yet through this stand of conviction, he was excommunicated.[2] He had wanted a return to the doctrine of justification by faith and a return to the Word of God's authority. He saw the need for the laity, as well as the clergy, to be educated.

Luther also committed an act that was considered in practice a great heresy. He translated the Bible into German so that the people could read it. Johannes Gutenberg was largely motivated to invent the printing press to allow literate people to read the Bible, his first publication. The Reformers believed in the necessity of educating people so they could read the Word of God. Thus, universal education again became an important goal.

There was a price on Luther's head, a judgment of death, but the Catholic Church was not able to stop the fire that Luther lit. King Charles V, proclaimed the Holy Roman Emperor, promised Luther safe passage so he could defend himself before the church council and the freedom to return the territory of the princes who supported the Reformation's doctrines in principle or for political purposes. (Some truly believed in Luther and the Reformation; others just wanted to lessen the power of the papacy and the emperor.)

Luther stood before the Diet of Worms. He did not know if Charles would keep his word. Church officials could have said, "We supersede the emperor's word," and regarded it as null and void. Luther defended the authority of the Scriptures

[2]   Hans J. Hillerbrand, "Martin Luther," *Encyclopedia Britannica*, vol. 25, (Chicago: Encyclopedia Britannica, 2007).

and the doctrine of justification by faith. He risked his life. He stood before the council and answered the accusations. Johann Eck, the prosecutor, emphasized that Luther stood against the authority of the princes, the ecumenical councils, and even the popes. It was a rejection of what had been taught throughout the years. Eck accused him of great arrogance.[3] Luther responded, "Unless I shall be convinced by the testimonies of the Scriptures or by clear reason... I neither can nor will make any retraction, since it is neither safe nor honorable to act against conscience." He also famously added, "Hier stehe ich. Ich kann nicht anders. Gott helfe mir. Amen" ("Here I stand. I can do no other. God help me. Amen)."[4]

The king kept his word, and Luther was given safe passage. Afterward, he was hunted from place to place. He died young in part because of the anxiety caused by the great attacks against him.

It's hard to keep my composure when I recount the story of Luther. This man performed one of the more courageous acts of history. Without it, we would not have the theology and understanding that we have today. God's way of working in history was bringing light in the midst of darkness, and the Reformation was a powerful light in what had been a dark time.

People have the capacity to do tremendous good and tremendous evil. Luther, so great before the Diet of Worms, did such evil in his later years. When Jews failed to respond to the Gospel during the Reformation, his anger was fueled against them. He was not a light to the Jewish people as the Lord commanded him to be. He lived in a culture that was antisemitic

[3] For a very good presentation of Johann Eck that supports his argument, see the older *Catholic Encyclopedia* (New York: Appleton Co, 1907).
[4] Hillerbrand, Hans J. "Martin Luther: Diet of Worms," *Encyclopedia Britannica*, vol. 25 (Chicago: Encyclopedia Britannica, 2007).
   Bainton, Roland, *Here I Stand: A Life of Martin Luther* (New York: Penguin, 1995), 60; Brecht, Martin, *Martin Luther*, tr. James L. Schaaf (Philadelphia: Fortress Press, 1985–93), 1:182; Kittelson, James, *Luther The Reformer* (Minneapolis: Augsburg Fortress Publishing House, 1986), 104.

and was taught to reject Israel according to that time's theological tradition. Luther is another example of God's partial and progressive restoration.

Justification by faith and the authority of Scripture for testing doctrine (*sola scriptura*) were the great things to come out of Luther, but Lutheranism was not the epitome of full restoration. Jewish roots were not restored to the Church partly because Rabbinic Judaism developed without the truths of the New Covenant Scriptures. Lutheranism remained very Gentile in appearances.

In the restoration process of the Church's Jewish roots, what is the first to be lost may be the last to be restored. There are glimmers of restored truth throughout history's dark days. However, there is no logical step-by-step reinstallation of what was lost. The Reformation was a positive step, but the minds behind the Reformation also produced fragmented groups with incompatible beliefs. In the beginning the fragmentation was not great, and it developed as people read God's Word and tried to understand it. They did not have the presence of the apostles to help with their misinterpretations, nor did they have an adequate understanding of the Bible's Jewish context.

Understanding the Bible in its Jewish context is very important for the sake of Church unity.[5] The people seeking truth had the Holy Spirit, but there was still pride and personal self-interest within the Reformation as well. There was not the humility and patience to stay together and pray toward unity and agreement. People began to interpret the Bible differently and came to various conclusions for restoration. The desire for an expedient truth became the foundation for mutual rejection.

The Reformers rightly taught that schism was a serious sin. Maintaining the unity of the Church was still a high ideal.

---

[5]   The context of Jewish roots is the only context able to release biblical unity to all areas of the Church in both understanding and experience. Every other attempt will eventually become a schism. Whenever unity is dealt with, the roots must always be addressed.

Rejecting those who teach false doctrine is appropriate, but the process must be slow and carefuly handled. In our quest for restoration and unity we need to listen and learn and not be quick to condemn.

The Eastern Orthodox Church

At the time of the Reformation there were two primary churches, the Eastern Orthodox Church and the Roman Catholic Church of the West. The split had come 450 years earlier, and a foundational issue for the split had been a disagreement regarding Jewish biblical roots. Although Eastern Orthodoxy also became antisemitic, repudiated some biblical Jewish tradtions, and adopted the replacement philosophy of covenant theology, they were more rooted in a Jewish calendar and the Bible's Jewish context.

One of the controversies between East and West went back to the second century over the use of the Jewish calendar or Roman solar calendar for Christian feasts. The Orthodox Church, especially in regard to Passover and the Resurrection, kept the Jewish calendar. Pope Victor of Rome argued with Polycrates, the bishop of Antioch. Polycrates wrote to Victor,

> "We observe the exact day; neither adding, nor taking away. For in Asia also great lights have fallen asleep, which shall rise again on the day of the Lord's coming, when he shall come with glory from heaven, and shall seek out all the saints. Among these are Philip, one of the twelve apostles, who fell asleep in Hierapolis; and his two aged virgin daughters, and another daughter, who lived in the Holy Spirit and now rests at Ephesus; and, moreover, John, who was both a witness and a teacher, who reclined upon the bosom of the Lord, and, being a priest, wore the sacerdotal plate. He fell asleep at Ephesus. And Polycarp in Smyrna, who was a bishop and martyr; and Thraseas, bishop and martyr from Eumenia, who fell asleep in Smyrna. Why need I mention the bishop and martyr Sagaris who fell asleep in Laodicea, or the blessed Papirius,

or Melito, the Eunuch who lived altogether in the Holy
Spirit, and who lies in Sardis, awaiting the episcopate
from heaven, when he shall rise from the dead? All these
observed the fourteenth day of the passover according
to the Gospel, deviating in no respect, but following the
rule of faith. And I also, Polycrates, the least of you all, do
according to the tradition of my relatives, some of whom
I have closely followed. For seven of my relatives were
bishops; and I am the eighth. And my relatives always
observed the day when the people put away the leaven.
I, therefore, brethren, who have lived sixty-five years in
the Lord, and have met with the brethren throughout the
world, and have gone through every Holy Scripture, am
not affrighted by terrifying words. For those greater than
I have said, 'We ought to obey God rather than man'...
I could mention the bishops who were present, whom I
summoned at your desire; whose names, should I write
them, would constitute a great multitude. And they, beholding my littleness, gave their consent to the letter,
knowing that I did not bear my gray hairs in vain, but
had always governed my life by the Lord Jesus."[6]

At Nicea I the East and West agreed on the calendar and
dating for Easter. However, new calendar revisions after Nicea
again produced tension between East and West.[7] The Orthodox
Church today often celebrates a different date for the Resurrection. Before the great split in East and West, the more primary issues were over matters of authority. This was especially so with
regard to the authority claimed by the Roman Catholic pope.[8]

Originally Church government was vested in elder plurality. However, what began as a plurality of elders with a head

---

[6]   Eusebius. *Church History*. Book V, Chapter 24.
[7]   For an excellent article on changes of dating after Nicea I again separating East and
West see the older *Catholic Encyclopedia*, vol. 27, 1908, 168 ff.
[8]   The seven-day week did not exist outside of the Jewish world in the first century.
The practice of taking Roman calendar holidays connecting them with Christian celebrations that were parallel to pagan misconceptions is understandable. Christians
were given these days off like other Romans but were not allowed to take Jewish days
off. However, in addition to synchronizing Roman holidays with Christian festivities,
the Church should have stressed the biblical days as the original context for the New
Covenant meanings. This is proper cultural adaptation.

elder (bishop) over each city evolved into the monarchical bishop over each city. The plurality of bishops together as a council over churches evolved into the primacy of the Roman bishop. The Eastern Orthodox Church, as manifested in the eleventh-century split from Rome, rejected this primacy of the Roman See. Eastern Orthodox people believed that they, not the Roman Church, were the true apostolic church. The Orthodox churches still maintain authority in patriarchs. They also hold to several doctrines that are troubling to Messianic Jews, such as the veneration of saints, worship through icons, and some ascetic practices.

The Reformation Under Calvin

Meanwhile, the light of the Reformation spread to different countries. Most noteworthy was the Reform Movement in Europe, which finds its basis in the writings of John Calvin. Calvin was inspired by Luther and was also a man of significant courage. Seeking to be true to Scripture, he wrote *Institutes of the Christian Religion.*[9]

The Calvinist Reformation in France and Switzerland later spread to Holland, England, and Scotland. In Scotland it was called *Presbyterianism,* meaning "government by elders."

Calvin talked about the Church being constantly re-formed.[10] Calvin asserted that our knowledge of truth is partial, as the Apostle Paul verifies, and forever in need of greater reformation.[11] Calvin's writings became the epitome of truth for the Reform Movement. However, the Reform Movement didn't always practice this worthy ideal!

---

[9]   He wrote it when he was twenty-six years old although he significantly revised it over the following years of his life. There is brilliance in *Institutes* that is truly astonishing. Many modern believers would be surprised to find doctrines ahead of their times in the ancient writers.

[10]   If you believe in fivefold ministry, Luther was apostolic in terms of what he was and did, but you will never have the biblical apostles who wrote Scripture and were eyewitnesses to Yeshua. You have intelligent people who lead Movements, oversee congregations, or plant multiple congregations, and people tend to camp around the truth that is restored by that leader's voice and do not go on to further restoration. The reverence given to the founding leader is often too great. His teaching becomes almost on par with Scripture.

[11]   John Calvin, *The Necessity of Reforming the Church* (Dallas: Protestant Heritage Press, 1995).

Calvin is usually known for his doctrine of predestination, known by the well-known acronym T-U-L-I-P, which stands for "Total depravity, Unconditional election, Limited atonement, Irresistible grace, and the Perseverance of the saints." I was well-schooled in Calvinism. I embraced Yeshua as a teenager in a Dutch Reformed Church in northern New Jersey. This included confirmation training under a pastor who was a traditional reformed amillennialist.[12] One time when I was in high school he said, "Oh brethren, let us hold onto this wonderful truth: whom God wills to save, He saves; and whom he wills to damn, he damns." Many people think, *Well, that's Calvinism.* However, that is only one part of it. To me it is a shame that Calvinism and the Reform Movement have been identified merely with a rigid predestinarianism that led to fatalism in hyper-Calvinists.

However, Calvinism was a twofold step in reclaiming the Church's Jewish roots. First, its understanding of biblical government was vested in a plurality of elders. This was much more akin to the first-century synagogal government and the government of the first-century Messianic Jewish Congregations. For Calvin there was one eldership in the church of the city that oversees all of the local gatherings. This is biblical. The second restoration in Calvinism was a significant understanding of the Kingdom of God. It was not the full understanding, but a vast improvement on the contemporary view. The Reform Movement continued to sharpen these views in later thinkers such as Abraham Kuyper, the prime minister of Holland at the turn of the century.[13] This re-forming of Kingdom thought continued into the work of George Ladd of Fuller

---

[12]   Amillennialism is the belief that the millennium (the one-thousand–year reign of Yeshua and the saints) is not a future event yet to come but is a present historical reality. The one thousand–year reign of believers began with the completed work of Yeshua on the cross and the one thousand years actually is an undesignated amount of time spanning from the cross to the Second Coming of Yeshua.

[13]   Abraham Kuyper became prime minister of Holland in 1901. A very good summary of his thoughts is in his *Lectures on Calvinism: Six Lectures Delivered at Princeton University 1898*, under the auspices of the L. P. Stone Foundation. Published today as Hendrickson Christian Classics, 2008.

Theological Seminary. Ladd has the best interpretation of the Kingdom to date.[14] All of the foundations for a true Kingdom understanding are found in John Calvin.

Sometimes the Kingdom of God was identified in Catholic thought as the institutional church, the Roman ecclesiastical organization per sé. Although this idea exists to some extent in Calvin, he identifies with a more biblical understanding of the Kingdom where people submit to the rule of God in every realm. Calvin understood that the Church preaches the Gospel of the Kingdom. The Good News is an invitation to come under the rule of the King through Yeshua's atonement, not the weak doctrine of grace taught in many of today's churches. Biblical grace always carries the sense of empowerment to obey God's commands.

In addition to restoring those two aspects, Calvin also had a high regard for the Law and moved the understanding closer to the original Jewish tradition of the early Church. He understood that believers were not under the Mosaic Covenant, but that the moral teachings of the whole Bible are enjoined as instruction to train us in righteousness (2 Timothy 3:16–17). Calvin taught that the Law's moral teachings do not have to be repeated in the New Testament to be enjoined, but Calvin used faulty criteria when contrasting the moral and ceremonial law. The differentiation between the moral and ceremonial is not as easily distinguished. For example, the Jewish way of life, as described by Moses, of the Sabbath, feasts, and food distinctions continues in the New Covenant order. We need to approach the teaching of Moses in the Spirit and ask, "How does each command apply in the New Covenantal order?" and "What is the Lord writing on my heart?" Calvinists understood that antinomianism, or anti-lawism, is a dangerous plague. Calvin did basically understand law and grace correctly

Calvin also taught a brilliant, revolutionary doctrine of vocation. This is a great restoration truth. Every believer has a vocation but does not have to be a full-time preacher to fulfill

14   *The Gospel of the Kingdom* by George Eldon Ladd.

a higher purpose. His vocation may be as ruler in civil government, an artist, an educator, an artisan, or an inventor. All legitimate vocations are equally callings of God. People were called to manifest the glory of God in their various vocations. All legitimate vocational calls are capable of manifesting God. God wants to embody the principles of his Kingdom rule in all realms of life. The businessman shows the Kingdom of God in the way he runs his business, as does the artist, the scientist, and the builder. The Calvinist concepts of culture are brilliant. This led to the understanding that it is not only full-time ministers who are to govern the churches. People in other vocations can be equally spiritual and can come into eldership to be church leaders as well as in other societal roles. The government of the Church became open to laity.

These were great restorations of truth in Calvinism, but did Calvin really understand Israel? No. Did he tend toward replacement theology? Yes. Did Calvin understand the millennial age—that there was a literal millennium? No. He still accepted the Catholic understanding of those things at that time.

Yet, there was still more truth to be restored.

5

Denominations and Streams

The Anabaptists

The Anabaptists believed that the Reformation did not go far enough.[1] There were two changes to Calvinism in Anabaptist theology. A person's theology will determine whether he or she believes that these changes are a restoration of truth. The Anabaptists—not to be confused with the Baptist church that is an offshoot of Puritanism—are the people we know today as the Mennonites, Amish, Church of the Brethren, and other Peace Churches.

First, the Anabaptists believed that infant baptism was not legitimate and taught that baptism was to be by immersion for only believing adults. I believe that baptism by immersion is one of the restorations steming from the Anabaptists (and later the Puritan Baptists). If you are an Anglican, Catholic, Presbyterian, or a Lutheran, you might not think that this was a restoration.[2]

Second, the Anabaptists had a different understanding of culture. The Calvinist understanding of culture was to bring God's rule into every area of life. The Anabaptists believed

---

[1]   Anabaptist means to *baptize again*.
[2]   I was an ordained Presbyterian. I used to argue for infant baptism. My Baptist wife said, "Well, your arguments sound good, but I don't sense it is right." And I'd say, "Let's go through the argument again!" Then I came into the Messianic Jewish world and studied the Jewish background of baptism. I came to the conclusion that she was right!

that the society was so corrupt that they had to create a total counterculture and disengage from society. The Anabaptists formed Peace Churches and were pacifists. According to their interpretation of the Sermon on the Mount, they did not believe that it was ever right for believers to go to war. There is a creative tension between the Anabaptists and the Reform views on engaging culture because the stance the Church—whether Anabaptist or Reform—can take is circumstantial. The Church in the United States historically and at the present time has taken the Reform stance. If you can invade the structures and change them through the Holy Spirit's leading, then do so because you can be politically involved. If under the Spirit you can take over educational structures and demonstrate the Kingdom's principles, you should do it. When there are enough believers living in holiness and love, then the culture can be influenced by their strength of witness. Sufficient numbers must support these efforts for change in conjunction with evangelism as a priority because it is an opportunity to witness.

The Church in the United States might soon lean more toward the Anabaptist stance, at least for a time, to purify the Church. Cultural institutions might become so crooked that we cannot involve ourselves in them to influence them without ourselves becoming corrupt. The world would then be too influential in the Church. If you cannot invade the structures of society without destroying your families, your lives, and the churches, then be more Anabaptist.

In some Anabaptist societies, however, there are major problems. The Amish became more of a works-righteousness society. Today, most believers with whom I have spoken and who live in Amish country say that the Amish do not understand justification by faith. Nonetheless, from my experience, the Mennonites and other Anabaptist streams are healthy expressions of biblical truth. They have something in common with the early Church, which was politically powerless, as well.

One of the glories of the Mennonites and other Anabaptists is that their pacifism kept them from persecuting the Jews. They were the first major movement of Christians institutionally that did not persecute the Jewish people. Some concepts of antisemitism might have existed, but their understanding of how to treat people with love was such that you cannot find, to my knowledge, any incident of Anabaptist persecution of the Jewish people.[3]

The Anglicans

The Reform Movement came into England when King Henry VIII did not want to be under the Catholic Church's authority because he wanted his marriage to a woman who could not produce a male heir annulled. The Church refused. He broke from the Catholic Church and became the head of the Church of England in an amazing union of church and state.

Evangelical Anglicans wanted a separation from the Roman Catholic Church for spiritual reasons. The Anglicans classified Lutheran, Reform, and Catholic views together. The Anglicans believed in apostolic succession[4] and the hierarchy of bishops. The doctrine of apostolic succession challenges the extreme position of American Christianity in which people appoint themselves to leadership merely by claiming God's call. Such leaders do not believe in accountability to a college of leaders or an accountable association of congregations. Should not real elders ordain new elders? In general does this not trace back to the apostolic ordination of elders? There is no warrant in Scripture for self-appointment to leadership and nonaccountability.

---

[3] A wonderful pro-Messianic Jewish position is found in the writings of the famous Mennonite New Testament theologian John Howard Yoder under the title *The Jewish Christian Schism Revisited*, (Grand Rapids: Eerdmans, 2003.) These were some of his last writings before his death. See pp. 43 ff. where he states that the separation of Judaism and Christianity and the rejection of Messianic Jews did not have to take place. History is fluid, and contrary to some in Jewish–Christian dialogue, this tradition of exclusion can be reversed.

[4] Apostolic succession is the doctrine that the apostles passed on their authority to the bishops of the early Church who in turn passed it on to the next generation. This doctrine affirms that apostolic authority today is found only in the bishops who are in direct succession from the original commission of the apostles. The Catholic, Eastern Orthodox, and Anglican communions hold to this doctrine.

Anglicans maintained a Catholic view of the Lord's Supper, which is called *transubstantiation* (the elements really become the literal body and blood of Yeshua), and held to the Lutheran doctrine of justification by faith, but were closer to the Calvinist view on other matters as explained in *The Thirty-Nine Articles*.[5]

The Puritans

As I study history, I realize that restoration is not a neat and simple progression. Many who believe in the restoration of the Church do not realize how much truth was taught in earlier periods of history. This becomes clear in a study of the Puritan Movement, one of the most extraordinary movements in Church history. The Puritans formed as a way to purify the Church. Some sought to work within the Church of England, and some became separatists, forming new independent congregations (Congregationalists) and some congregations in association (Presbyterians). Puritans had a great knowledge of Scripture, and some of their writings contain some very modern scholarship. One example is William Gurnell's *The Christian in Complete Armour*. (After the death of Oliver Cromwell, England's Puritan leader in the seventeenth century, Gurnell became an Anglican, but his theology was Puritan.) It was written in the mid-1600s and is amazingly relevant for today.

Some Puritans experienced extraordinary visitations of the Holy Spirit and entered into amazing depths of prayer and revival. Some of these visitations' descriptions appear in the writings of Ian Murray. One recorded, "Ten men fell down during our prayer meeting last night, and they remained as dead all night long." They did not fully understand it. They continued, "We carried them out of the meeting, and the next day they told of dreams and visions of wonderful things that they had seen in the heavenlies." These kinds of things were not rare in Puritan prayer meetings, but few are aware of this history.

---

[5]   *The Thirty-Nine Articles* is the basic confession of faith for the Anglican Church (Episcopal in America).

Some among the Puritans were the first to clearly teach and write on the restoration of ethnic Israel. Not all of the Puritans saw it because, with their foundation in Reform theology, some followed Calvin on this point. However, in general, they maintained an amazingly positive heart toward the Jewish people. The Puritans who came from England to America understood themselves as living out deliverance in a role parallel to that of Israel. The crossing of the sea paralleled the exodus from Egypt. Their colonies were seen as a new Israel. In the thinking of many Puritans, this was not replacement theology. The Puritans wanted to be a nation among nations that was a light just as Israel had been meant to be. The phrase "city on a hill," a Puritan ideal of John Winthrop, needs to be understood in its Puritan context. For some this was a replacement of ethnic Israel, but for others it was a complement or in addition to ethnic Israel. They truly wanted to be a New Covenant biblical society.

The Puritans of England actually replaced the monarchy and took over the government of England in 1649 under the protectorate of Oliver Cromwell. It is a remarkable thing to realize that the Puritans did rule England for a time and founded a nation in America.[6]

Another contribution of the Puritans was their belief that the Law of God was to inform society—society had to conform with God's rule. They progressed toward republican government due to their understanding of plurality of elders and the priesthood of believers. Elders were elected and accountable to an educated adult membership of a local congregation. The Puritans, however, did not rightly distinguish civil and religious government in the colonies. They depended upon the civil government to enforce Church doctrinal fidelity. Roger

---

[6] The democratic republic format of government in the United States was partially rooted in Puritan writings. Plurality, the philosophy behind Calvinists' Church government, was the predecessor of the American Revolution and political freedom. The British called the American Revolution the *Presbyterian Revolution*. Enlightenment writers John Locke and Montesquieu and by Presbyterian Church government strongly influenced the writing of the Constitution. It is amazing that we don't study these things in our schools. These are truths well documented by historians.

Williams, the Baptist founder of Rhode Island, was closer to the truth in distinguishing civil and church government.

Some of the Puritans saw that the Church was called to make ethnic Israel jealous and felt that the Church's history in regard to the Jewish people was terrible. Puritans invited the Jews from all over Europe to come to the English colonies for refuge. The United States' policy of favoring the Jewish people comes from the Puritan insight concerning Israel. We think of Reform theology as being replacement theology, but this was not so among many of the Puritans. Samuel Rutherford, the author of *Lex Rex*,[7] wrote the most poignant words of love concerning Yeshua's heart toward the Jewish people. "When they find each other again," he wrote, "how they will embrace and weep together!" Puritans believed that by being a new Israel and a city set on a hill, they had to show compassion to old Israel. Some of them, a minority, even believed that the Jewish people needed to be restored to the land of Israel. The majority believed that they had a role in showing compassion to Israel, opposing antisemitism and playing a Romans 11 role in making Israel desirous of faith in Yeshua. Increase Mather, the president of Harvard, wrote a book on Romans 9–11 and the restoration of national Israel.[8] The writings of the Puritans influenced Anglican Bishop Joseph Butler in England. In 1732 he wrote that we can expect that all of the promises to the Jewish people, even their return to their land, to be fulfilled. His apologetic text, *The Analogy of Religion*, which for 150 years was the basic textbook of apologetics in English-speaking seminaries and schools, popularized this concept.

Unfortunately, Puritan influence and power in England declined, and the restored monarchy with Catholic leanings stifled Puritan influence. Even in that darkness, the Puritans

---

[7]   *Law is King* by Samuel Rutherford was a great treatise on government being accountable to law and calling for democratic directions.

[8]   It is false to teach that the belief in the Jewish people's destiny was the creation of J. N. Darby and his dispensationalist followers in the nineteenth and twentieth centuries.

came to believe in the Church's restoration to unity and righteousness. The Puritans will always be remembered for their courage, fervor, zeal for revival, and call to holiness. Did they understand all of God's healing promises, the gifts of the Holy Spirit, and fivefold ministry? No. Some were amillennial, some were postmillennial, and some did not clearly articulate a millennial view. They did believe that a succession of revivals would bring many to faith worldwide before the Lord's coming. During that last great call to faith, the Church would come to a place of glory whereby Israel would be made jealous, restored, and re-engrafted. Some believed in the restoration of the Church and Israel together. As far back as the 1600s, these restoration theories were circulating.

Christians and Messianic Jews today would benefit from reading Ian Murray's *The Puritan Hope*, a book that does not see Israel quite as a literal restoration. Dr. Michael Brown in his book on antisemitism, *Our Hands Are Stained with Blood*, has a chapter on Christians and the churches that treated Jewish people well. There were times in both Israel's history and Church history where God's people were faithful. The Jews were faithful during David's reign and the early years of Solomon. This is true of Church history as well. We need to judge the history of the Church regarding Israel, fairly.

The Baptists in England are an offshoot of the Puritan Movement. They were Puritan in doctrine and government at least in the beginning. In England, the Presbyterian Movement eventually predominated among Puritans. The colonial Puritans had a more democratic orientation until the Presbyterian influence from England invaded. Congregationalists lost their evangelical doctrines and some became Unitarians. The separation came when Baptists rejected Calvinist baptism doctrine in favor of immersion only for adults (or at least those who could make a true decision for Yeshua), and a powerful worldwide movement began. Baptists eventually became more democratic in structure, with the pastor as the elder and the deacons as the board.

The Moravians and the Methodists

The Puritan Movement declined at the end of the seventeenth and the beginning of the eighteenth centuries. The fervor of the Spirit was lost. Like many movements, it became an intellectual system that people affirmed.[9] A subsequent movement of restoration was the Moravian Movement, which paved the way for the Methodists. The Moravians were restorationists who sought to purify the Church in Central Europe. They were severely persecuted under the Hapsburgs. Some came to Hernhutt, Germany, to plead with Count Nikolaus Ludwig von Zinzendorf to become their leader.

The story of Zinzendorf is important. A German movement called *Lutheran Pietism,* with its foundation in English Puritan writings, a deep return to Scripture, and a strong commitment to the Jewish people and their salvation, had influenced Zinzendorf. Zinzendorf's heart burned for revival, the unity of the Church, and world missions. He started a community called Hernhutt to further these ends. All who truly confessed Yeshua and sought to do his will were welcome.

This amazing community was filled with singing; countless hymns were composed. A twenty-four–hour prayer meeting was in continuous operation. It lasted for a hundred years. Moravian missionaries went throughout the world to bring people to Yeshua. They signed on to row in ship galleys to lead the galley slaves to Yeshua. They were martyred in tribal lands. When Zinzendorf sent missionaries where churches existed, they would not plant a Moravian church but got the other churches to embrace cooperative unity if they could.

---

[9] However, there was a great Puritan revival during the days of Jonathan Edwards in the 1740s. Based on Romans 11, Edwards argued for a great future hope for the Jewish people. We continue to see a succession of restorations and revivals. During a revival there is often a rediscovery of the Bible's teaching of a place for Israel. Edwards bridged two great Movements of restoration through his friendship with George Whitefield. John Wesley printed part of Edwards' defense of the New England Revival in the 1740s.

The original Moravians, who were excommunicated by the Catholic Church and slaughtered by the Hapsburgs, embraced the doctrine of apostolic succession. Therefore, Moravian leaders encouraged Zinzendorf to seek ordination to carry on this succession; he did so. He could say to Lutherans that he believed in justification by faith. To the churches who believed in apostolic succession, he could profess to believe in succession. To the Presbyterians, he could say he believed in government by a plurality of elders. He actually did join all of this together. In addition, Zinzendorf established the centrality of the small group meeting for accountability, discipleship, and mutual prayer. However, most amazing was his embracing of the Jewish people. This was so deep that Zinzendorf's emissaries planted the first Messianic Jewish congregation in the 1740s in Amsterdam. Archives discovered by Lutheran Pastor Bender in Austria list members, show sketches of a Messianic Jewish wedding, and more.[10] Rabbis were secretly members.

Many attribute the beginning of modern Protestant missions to the Moravians because of the foundation in their prayer meetings and their sending many to the field. Zinzendorf was one of the greatest figures in Protestant Church history because he anticipated much of what we believe about restoration.

Influenced by the Moravians, the Methodist restoration was one of the greatest in history. Two great apostolic figures, George Whitefield, the Calvinist, and John Wesley, the Armenian, led it. Wesley himself was led to an experiential faith through the witness of a Moravian. He said that his heart was strangely warmed when he came to faith. The Methodists saw a restoration of the Spirit in their great evangelistic campaigns. They also restored the centrality of small groups as the method of discipleship and raising up new leaders. Methodism got its name from this pattern. (Again, some things thought to be recently restored were actually present years before.)

---

[10] I have personally seen copies of these archival documents that list events and members.

During the days of John Wesley, Methodists were Anglicans. They did not desire to leave the mother church in England. Most classical denominations formed because people were not allowed to practice the truth they discovered in Scripture and were eventually forced to leave. This was true of Lutheran, Reformed, Anabaptist, Methodist, and other believers. In the old days people thought it a grievous thing to divide. Schism was to be avoided if at all possible. Today, there are thousands of denominations and streams. To many it is a badge of honor to set up your own group, whether an independent congregation or a denomination.

What did Methodism believe? Wesley saw the need for people to have a personal conversion experience and to encounter the Holy Spirit, reaffirming some of the Puritan emphases. Wesley also believed in small group discipleship and accountability. In the small group they asked each other, "How goes your spiritual life? How is your devotional life, victory over sin, and your evangelistic witness?" Men were discipled and raised to lead new groups. With this emphasis people were sent out to preach the Gospel and plant new groups. It was basically what is known today as the *cell group structure,* or the G12 structure.

Wesley never wanted to leave the Anglicans. He was raising up lay pastors and leaders to add to the Anglican program. The Anglican hierarchy saw this as a negative. They wanted only the ordained clergy to preach the Gospel. After Wesley's death, the Methodists were forced out. They still kept a government hierarchy more like Anglicanism with ordained bishops but not apostolic succession. The small group orientation continued for some years after Wesley. When they came to the United States, the Methodists became the nineteenth century's most important revival movement. Combined with the moving of the Spirit, the small group method raised up countless church planters, which is why in most towns and hamlets there is a Methodist church.[11] The Methodists were winning

---

[11]   Today, the Methodist church has largely apostatized. The onslaught of evolution theory and secular humanism in the nineteenth century swept through the Methodist seminaries at the turn of the century.

converts because there were camp meetings, revival meetings, street preaching, teaching sessions, small groups, camps at the seashore, and camps in the woods. The Presbyterians, the people of the previous restoration, were offended, saying of the lay preachers, "They are not educated. They have not a seminary degree," because the earlier restoration tends to look down on the new restoration.

Charles Finney originally was a Presbyterian, but he defended the Methodists. Finney held that although Presbyterians were looking down at those Methodists for their lack of education, they were doing the work. They are winning the world![12] Their small group discipleship method was the greatest evangelistic force in nineteenth-century America. The Methodist Movement was really a restoration of the Spirit and of the biblical pattern of small groups and accountability.

The Methodists also believed in a doctrine of perfection where you could dedicate your life so as not to sin again called *entire sanctification*. This belief has generally not been embraced since early Methodism. The twentieth-century Methodists also gave up the small group method, one of the patterns that gave them their name, but they kept the name *Methodist* anyway.

The Beginnings of Christian Zionism

The Anglican–Lutheran Move Toward Unity and Israel

In the nineteenth century Frederick William IV, the king of Prussia (today's Germany), was studying the Word of God. There were truly spiritual people around him. The Moravians and Lutheran Pietists had influenced some of them. Real revivals are frequently noted by a concern for Israel. Frederick believed, on the basis of John 17, that the evangelical church needed to unite and become one. He came to believe that the

---

[12]   See Nathan Hatch, *The Democratization of American Christianity* (New Haven: Yale University Press, 1989), 189. This theme of spiritual power against mere eduction (though Finney was not against eduction, per se), is found in his *Lectures on the Revival of Religion* (Cornwall: Diggory Press, 2007).

Protestant Church should engage in a unifying project as an expression of biblical truth. Indeed, he believed that the unity of the Church would lead to the Jewish people's salvation. The project was to establish a saved remnant of Israel in Israel in preparation for the Jew's great return as predicted by the prophets.[13] Establishing this saved remnant would lead to the revelation of God's glory and Yeshua's return. Frederick embraced the Lutheran Pietist and Puritan theology, some of which held to proto-Christian Zionists views.

Frederick assigned a leading Lutheran to contact the Anglican Church's Archbishop of Canterbury to put forth the case that all evangelical believers needed to unite for a mission to reach out to Israel. He offered to give the Anglicans primacy in this mission because the Anglicans had both Lutheran and Reform roots. They had the opportunity to be a united force and could be trusted for leadership. Lutherans argued that they needed to have a mission to Israel and establish a Protestant presence in the land. This would establish a new Jewish Christian presence in the ancient land of promise, considered a necessary prelude to the Second Coming of Yeshua.

When the Prussian theologians dialogued with the Anglican theologians, Frederick's emissaries found England already committed to restoration of Israel. They visited Queen Victoria, the symbolic head of the Anglican Church, and she too became convinced. In England, because the church and state are not separated as in America, they went to the Parliament. Parliament passed the Israel mission as legislation in the 1840s.[14] They did not understand Messianic Jewish expression as we do now, but they planned something with some similar features. They decided to try to find a Jew whom they could train to become the Protestant bishop in Jerusalem. This, they

[13] For an account of Frederick IV and these concepts see Kevin Crombie, *A Jewish Bishop in Jerusalem* (Jerusalem: Nicolayson's Ltd., 2006), 70 ff. Also sections in Franz Koebler, *The Vision Was There* (London: World Jewish Congress, 1954).
[14] See Crombie, 80 ff. for Queen Victoria's support and Parliment legislation passed in August 1841.

believed, would begin a movement in Jerusalem of the saved remnant of Israel.

In general, they also wanted to encourage Jewish people to go back to Israel. They saw themselves as players in fulfilling biblical prophecy. It is amazing to note that Christianity in Britain by 1840 was Zionist in perspective. Baptists, Methodists, Anglicans, and many Presbyterians were in agreement, which was why the legislation passed.

God does his work through his instruments. We can see here the beginnings of Christian Zionism. If it had not been for Christian Zionists, there would probably be no Jewish state today. The plan was carried out, and Bishop Michael Solomon Alexander was appointed to Jerusalem. Bishop Alexander was the son of a rabbi and well trained in Rabbinic Judaism. As a young man he embraced Yeshua and became a worker with the Anglican mission to the Jews.[15] Norwegian Lutherans put up considerable funds for his work.

Ultimately, however, the non-Protestant groups in Israel thwarted the plans. Turkey ruled Palestine. The Orthodox and Catholics expected Turkey to keep the Protestants out, making this an international affair. Bishop Alexander died a few years later, but an Anglican Church called Christ Church, which is the church that was planted then, still survives inside the Joppa Gate. Due to political pressures, the Jewish bishopric did not continue, but the church did, and today, a Messianic Jewish congregation meets in that building.

The Jewish community does not see the great importance that Christian Zionists played in the establishing of the state of Israel. The theology mentioned earlier was instrumental in bringing many people to support establishing the nation of Israel. In the nineteenth century the earl of Shaftesbury became prominent in Christian Zionist endeavors. Arthur John Balfour, the British foreign secretary and a Christian Zionist, was responsible for the Balfour Declaration of 1917. The Balfour

---

[15]   Crombie provides a very full biography of Michael Solomon Alexander.

Declaration declared it British policy that Palestine was to be the homeland for the Jewish people shortly before the League of Nations mandated that Palestine be given into British trusteeship.[16] Later, Great Britain went back on this declaration. In the 1930s, British Major John Wingate, a passionate Christian Zionist, is credited with training the Haganah, the Jewish people's defense force in Palestine, to defend themselves against the attacks of the Arab marauders before Israel became a state.[17] This force became the Israel Defense Force after the state of Israel's creation.

Even powerful figures in the United States were involved in Christian Zionist work. Who from the United States greatly encouraged Theodor Herzl, the father of the Jewish state? It was W. E. Blackstone, another Christian Zionist. Blackstone was a Christian missionary to the Jews in Chicago and founded the American Messianic Fellowship.[18] He influenced U.S. policy to favor the Zionist cause. An Anglican chaplain at the British Embassy in Vienna, Reverend William Hechler was also a Christian Zionist and close confidant who encouraged Herzl in his endeavors.[19]

God's workings are wonderful. Every seed sown in prayer and godly effort will add up; the total force of it will be a key to save Israel in the Last Days. The prayers of all Christians from history will have their effect. There will be a generation that will see the triumph of the Kingdom of God, and the promise of Romans 11:25, 26 will come to pass.

---

[16] For Balfour's Christian Zionist upbringing and motives, see sections in Koebler.

[17] For a full account of Wingate, see John Bierman and Colin Smith, *Fire in the Night* (New York: Random House, 1999).

[18] For information on William Blackstone see the website of American Messianic Fellowship in Chicago where a short biography is available. www.lifeinmessiah.org.

[19] See Jamie Cowen, *The Untold Story* www.leader.org, July 2002. Cowen is the recent president of the Union of Messianic Jewish Congregations. His account is also dependent on Koebler's sections on Chaplain Hechler. www.leaderu.org.

6

Restoration Movements in the United States–Nineteenth and Twentieth Century

Because the European churches were state churches, the same multiplication of denominations does not exist in countries outside of the United States as found inside the United States. The separation of civil and religious governments gave an opportunity of unparalleled freedom, but America's founding fathers never intended to separate civil government from responsibility to God. Such a separation is a false doctrine.

Unfortunately, many Jewish people think that they are safest in a secular state. The Declaration of Independence notes that man's rights come from God. Every person's worth is rooted in belief in God. This was the consensus of nineteenth-century America and Britain. It is right for the state to acknowledge God and embrace a basic law rooted in God. This is the reason the words *under God* were added to the Pledge of Allegiance and why *In God we trust* is on our coins. This does not mean that there is not religious liberty. Religiously inspired crimes provide the only reason for limitations. A person is free to be an atheist. However, the state should acknowledge a basic belief in God and accountability to God as its orientation. A secular state will ultimately turn on Jewish people because of an insufficient value commitment to maintain true compassion for others and the sacred worth of all human beings. Only a biblically minded people will provide safe haven for Jews. True biblical faith contains a moral motivation to not fall into persecuting any man made in the image of God. Non-state churches have never persecuted the Jewish people. In the interest of religious freedom, the United States gave unprecedented freedom and equality to all religious denominations that people desired to form.

In this environment of religious freedom, the concept of restoration became very prominent in the nineteenth century. Some saw the restoration of the Church as a Last Days' priority. People spoke of creating or restoring true New Testament churches. These movements were trying to return to greater purity in New Testament Church government, New Testament holiness, and New Testament empowerment. There were visitations of the Spirit in these new movements' gatherings. Because of their doctrine and convictions concerning biblical government, some were forced to leave the structures or denominations in which they held membership. New denominations were formed. The fragmentation of the Body is concerning, but much of the forgotten truth was also now being understood.

Most denominations in the nineteenth century came into existence because a group of people came to deep convictions about particular issues. Many times, they were not allowed to practice their convictions in the structures that existed, and so they had to go outside of the camp to practice restoration truths. In the seventeenth century the Baptists had to go outside of the Puritan camp to practice adult believer baptism by immersion. In the nineteenth century when different people began to see what they perceived to be restoration truths, sometimes their views were right and sometimes they were wrong. The new free churches in Europe believed in freedom from state control and left state structures to practice restoration truth. It is my conviction that schism is serious sin. People should not create new denominations and splits unless they are precluded from practicing what they consider important convictions.

The Seventh Day Movement

The Seventh Day Movement reflected the conviction that restoration required the Church to keep the seventh day as the Sabbath.[1] The Seventh Day people believed that they were restoring New Testament Christianity by worshipping on the seventh day. The Adventists were one group of Seventh Day people. Ellen G. White, who claimed to be a prophetess, was their leader. She claimed to have received a revelation that the Lord would return in 1848, but of course this did not come to pass. She then claimed that he had partially returned to the court of the tabernacle in heaven for an investigative judgment, but not yet to earth. The Seventh Day Adventists saw a high place for the Law and even obeyed the biblical food laws. It is strange that the Sabbath became so important, yet the other feasts were not emphasized, which was partly due to the Sabbath command's inclusion in the Ten Commandments.

The Adventists saw themselves as the new Israel; they did not see a role for natural Israel. Adventists also believed that to worship on Sunday was a mark of the beast, the Antichrist, which produced a separation from other Christians. Some leading people in the Seventh Day Adventist Movement, for example, Seventh Day Baptists, today do not take such extreme positions.

The Church of God and Church of Christ Movements

Other movements of restoration included the Church of God (Anderson, Indiana), the Church of Christ (known for singing without musical instruments), and the Disciples of

---

[1] My own understanding is that there is an accommodation in this transitional age to not require the Sabbath for all Christians. However, there is no biblical command for Sabbath's replacement by Sunday either. In the Age to Come the whole world will be seventh day oriented.

Christ. Many were reading the Word and seeking restoration but coming to different conclusions. The Nazarenes and the Christian and Missionary Alliance were formed as well to more closely express New Testament truth. By the end of the nineteenth century and due to the multiplication of denominations, most of the possible interpretations of the Bible within Christian Protestant orthodoxy were represented. Many were interpreting the Bible without sufficient carefulness and humility, leading to unnecessary fragmentation.

The Holiness Movement

The Holiness Movement was also a great movement of restoration, which began to see Israel's importance. Known for their camp meetings and successful missionary endeavors, there was a commitment to revival and world missions. Many have rightfully expressed concern that these movements tended to legalism; however, there was also great sincerity and piety.

A. B. Simpson and A. J. Gordon are two examples. They founded Nyack College and Gordon College, respectively. These were significant movements of the Holy Spirit under apostolic men. Simpson and Gordon taught that physical healing was part of the blessing of the New Covenant, and Simpson wrote a book on the subject. He also accepted the reality of the gifts of the Spirit. Andrew Murray, a South African Presbyterian, wrote a book on healing as well. Dispensationalists spoke well of these authors but did not distribute their books on healing or the gifts of the Spirit.[2] The Holiness Movement spawned the Nazarenes, the Christian Missionary Alliance, new Methodist groups, and Pentecostal denominations and impacted some of the older Methodist groups.

---

[2]   Dispensationalists to some degree don't believe they are under the Mosaic order. However, the question is how boundaries are drawn or dispensations defined. I do not agree with how dispensationalism makes distinctions. We are all reformed, too. We are reformed and reforming.

The Pentecostal Movement

At the end of the nineteenth century, while one part of the Church was experiencing significant advances, many of the denominations began to apostatize as evolutionary ideas and humanistic orientations began to make major inroads into seminaries. This fed the decline of the old denominations to this day. In the beginning of the twentieth century, the Pentecostal revival took place, which grew out of the Holiness Movement, paralleling the early Zionist movement and Herzl's Zionist Congress. The Holiness movement largely believed in the gifts of the Holy Spirit but lacked clarity in definition. The Pentecostal revival embraced the Second Blessing doctrine of the Holiness movement believed by Holiness, Wesleyan, Nazarene, and Alliance people.[3]

The Pentecostal Movement became a great movement. It did not begin with great numbers, but the Pentecostal Movement is one of the greatest forces in world missions. God was doing something through this movement. Non-Pentecostals claimed that Pentecostals were heretics because they spoke in tongues. The Nazarene denomination made speaking in tongues an offense requiring discipline. Some even claimed that speaking in tongues was "of the devil." The Pentecostal's response was to claim that other Christians were not baptized in the Holy Spirit because they did not speak in tongues. Those within the Holiness ranks were greatly divided.

By the end of the 1920s, the Pentecostals had organized into associations. They had formed denominations (some do not like to use this word) to further their movement. God was restoring the functions of the Holy Spirit's gifts and power. The Church of God in Christ was formed and then the

---

[3] The Second Blessing refers to the baptism of the Holy Spirit. However, Pentecostalism taught that you did not have this experience unless you spoke in tongues. I believe in speaking in tongues, but you cannot prove that this is because of the baptism of the Holy Spirit. Both Moody and Torrey believed in the baptism of the Holy Spirit. They were part of the Holiness movement. I do believe that those baptized in the Spirit can speak in tongues, but it does not necessarily follow that you do not have the baptism of the Spirit without speaking in tongues.

Assemblies of God. Later, the Pentecostal Holiness denomination and the Church of God of Cleveland, Tennessee, were formed. There were differences in government and practices among Pentecostal groups. One denomination also formed was the heretical United Pentecostal Church. They believed that Yeshua and the Father were the same person. When Yeshua was praying to the Father, he was simply praying to his higher self. This group was looked down upon by other Pentecostal churches.

The Apostolic Church, another denomination, which was strong in Australia, taught the restoration of fivefold ministry in function and government (apostles, prophets, evangelists, pastors, and teachers). Due to racial divisions, the Assembly of God separated from its black brothers in the Church of God in Christ, the largest Pentecostal denomination in America today.

The Dispensational Movement: A Repudiation of the Restoration of the Last Days Church

A movement came about in the nineteenth century that was a restoration of some truths. This movement was the Plymouth Brethren Movement in England under John Darby, who gave the world *dispensational theology*.[4] The Plymouth Brethren sought to restore the priesthood of all believers. Elders in plurality governed their assemblies. The distinction between clergy and laity was transcended. There are few truly classical dispensationalists today, but the influence of dispensational theology in America is still very strong, and much revision to the theory is currently taking place.

John Darby, who was a great influence on the *Scofield Reference Bible*, saw deadness in the Anglican Church. One of his

---

[4]   Dispensational theology is a scheme of biblical interpretation that divides history into several distinct eras, or dispensations. Although according to Scofield there are seven dispensations, generally dispensationalism is understood as emphasizing three (OT dispensation of law, present dispensation of grace, and the future dispensation of the millennial kingdom following the second advent of Christ).

emphases—a key part of Brethren theology—was that there should be an educated laity, a plurality of elders, who would lead the Church.

Darby also taught that communion should be only for those who were righteous members of a Brethren group. These groups were called Closed Brethren. Those from other denominations could not participate. The Closed Brethren influenced Watchman Nee, the famous leader of the Chinese Church in the first half of the twentieth century. Nee could not abide by their separatism. Those who wanted greater openness formed Open Brethren assemblies.

The Brethren came to a very strong belief in the restoration of Israel. The literal future millennium (premillennialism) is also a very strong and positive teaching of dispensationalism. Dispensationalism defined the millennial age and the reality of Israel in the greatest clarity that had been seen since the apostolic age.

On the other hand, dispensationalism put forth distinctions that are very problematic. Darby defined a doctrine of grace (which is still taught by some today) whereby a person can be saved without submitting to Yeshua's Lordship, a radically different understanding of salvation by grace. In dispensationalism you can accept Yeshua as Savior but not necessarily receive him as Lord and also repent from sin. They argued that receiving him as Lord is a separate and subsequent decision that is unnecessary for salvation; otherwise, salvation would be by works.

When I was a youngster, I attended Word of Life Camp in Upstate New York under Reverend Jack Wyrtzen's direction. This was a major discipling influence in my life for which I am forever grateful. I can remember that they would preach salvation Saturday, Sunday, Monday, and Tuesday. The philosophy was "What have you got to lose? Say the prayer, and go to heaven." No life change was required. After Tuesday the teaching changed. The emphasis was that you could continue to sin, not commit your life to the Lord, and still go to heaven, but you would be miserable if you did not commit your life.

"How can you not commit your life to walk in the light of the One who was crucified for you?" Wednesday, Thursday, and Friday they tried to get everybody to commit their lives to the Lord. There were campfire dedication meetings. They presented two different experiences: one salvation and one dedication because if you have to accept Yeshua as Lord to be saved, then grace is not grace.

They understood grace as undeserved favor from God. However, they lost sight of a dimension of grace. It is empowerment to believe in God and submit to the rule of the King. Biblical grace carries the power of obedience. You cannot receive grace if you intend to live in sin. The Gospel is the undeserved invitation to come back into the Father's house under his rule as King (Luke 15). Grace is the empowerment to obey the Word.

In dispensationalism, language about salvation was changed. Early nineteenth-century evangelists spoke about the number of people who made "professions of faith." In Calvinism, whether they were saved was proven by whether they brought forth fruit, making their calling and election sure. In Arminianism , the profession was proven as true by the holy life of fruitfulness. They never said that a person had been saved in their meeting, but that a person had made a profession of faith. In contrast, dispensationalism said that a person was saved at their meetings. According to this theology, you could be saved, never produce real fruit, and still go to heaven. Their doctrine of grace was such that simply praying the prayer was enough. You might never see the person again; they might never join in fellowship, but if he or she believed and said the "Sinner's Prayer," he or she was saved. Not all dispensationalists believe this today.[5]

---

[5]   We must become much more aware of the realities of language. When we say that a person was saved at a meeting, do we recognize the implications? *Language either reveals reality or conceals reality*. It is important. We should note that dispensationalists did require a standard of holiness for church membership and emphasized holy living. They truly wanted people to dedicate their lives to the Lord and receive the life of joyful service available to them.

Dispensationalism taught that the Spirit's supernatural gifts were not of this age but only of the period before Scripture was given. Despite this, the other features of dispensationalism swept the Pentecostal Movement in the 1920s, and many Bible schools and Christian colleges also became dispensational. There were other distinctions as well. The Old Testament era was considered a dispensation of Law, which contrasted with New Covenant as a dispensation of grace. Distinctions were made between Israel and the Church, whereby if you were a part of Israel, then you were part of the Covenant of Law, which would be reestablished in the millennial age for Israel. If you were a part of the Church, then you were a part of the Covenant of Grace.[6]

In classical dispensationalism, Israel and the Church have to be separated. Originally, in dispensationalism, a Jewish believer could not live a Jewish life because to do so was considered a confusion of the dispensations. At the turn of the century, when Zionism was in its early years, a small movement had begun that was called the Messianic Jewish Movement. It had started with a journal, *The Hope of Israel*, edited by Arno C. Gabelein and Gerald Stroker. These two men had started a mission to the Jews in New York, and Gabelein had once preached in Yiddish to one thousand Orthodox Jews. Gabelein had called for the formation of Messianic congregations. Gabelein and Stroker had agreed with others such as Theodore Luckey, who edited *The Messianic Jew*, who had been calling for such a Jewish distinction. Luckey was an Adventist in Eastern Europe. Joseph Rabinowitz in Kishinev, Moldava, was also an important leader for this Messianic Jewish direction. [7]

---

[6] My understanding is that both the Mosaic and New Covenants are gracious covenants, but because grace without the Holy Spirit's fullness, as found under the Mosaic Covenant, was not adequate, God took more of the responsibility to fulfill the covenant through the Holy Spirit and the promise of writing the Law in the hearts of Israel and Judah (Jeremiah 31:31). I am more Reformed in regard to the Law and grace, but I am more dispensational in regard to the role of Israel in the millennial age. Some call this view *covenant premillennialism.*

[7] This is according to the archived editions of *The International Hebrew Christian Alliance* journals. Also, for Rabinowitz, see the masterful biography by Kai Kjaer-Hansen, *Joseph Rabinowitz* (Grand Rapids: Eerdmans, 1994).

Gabelein broke from his ministry and his participation with others in these hopeful trends because he read dispensational theology and became convinced that he had been wrong.[8] He rejected the idea of Jews living a Jewish life in the New Covenant and being both a Christian and a Jew as a part of the Bride and the earthly Israel. He came to believe that if you are born a Jew, become a believer in Yeshua, and are still living as part of the destiny of Israel, then you have confused the dispensations. You are either a part of the Bride of Messiah or part of Israel; you cannot be part of both.

Gabelein became a famous dispensational theologian, becaming one of the key editors of the *Scofield Reference Bible* that summarized dispensational teaching. Stroker, his partner, did not agree with these dispensational distinctions. He so passionately disagreed that he went back to Germany to continue the work.

Those in Jewish missions who were influenced by classical dispensationalism sometimes planted Hebrew Christian churches. If they were classical dispensationalists, they did not keep Passover. They might have had a picture of the *seder* table in the sanctuary for sentimental reasons. Some had a Passover meal demonstration for its teaching value. However, it was considered wrong to actually have a Passover *seder* meal. In a way, those churches were halfway houses toward the assimilation of Jews into gentile Christianity.

Dispensationalism was wrong about the relationship between the covenants. This movement presented its teaching with great clarity and power so that some of its weaknesses were overlooked. The dispensationalists restored some aspects of New Testament government and doctrine. However, they lost the Puritan hope of the true Church being restored to John 17 unity, power, and holiness. They were pessimistic about the Last Days' Church, which they believed would be raptured out before the seven-year tribulation. They did

---

[8] See the account in David Rausch, *Zionism in Early American Fundamentalism* (Lewiston: Mellon Press, 1978).

not emphasize the restoration of the body. In the twentieth century, waiting for an impending rapture became the focus. The Puritan idea of the Christian lifestyle influencing vocations and all of culture was lost. The prevailing thought was, *Why save a sinking ship?* The view that bearing witness to the Kingdom expedites Yeshua's return was also lost.

The Theology of George Ladd: His Impact on My Life

My spiritual father, who was the dearest, most saintly man I have ever known, was the late Chaplain Evan Welsh of Wheaton College. He nursed my wife, Patty, and me back to faith through our own times of personal crisis. He was both a Presbyterian and like a nineteenth-century Holiness person. He loved the teachings of Christian and Missionary Alliance leaders, such as A. B. Simpson and A. W. Tozer. Chaplain Welsh was a man of great godliness, who was continually manifesting the presence of God. His father had been the pastor of College Church in Wheaton. (Although not affiliated with Wheaton College, it was called College Church because it was right across the street from the campus.)

College Church became divided over dispensational theology. Previously, they had taught a classical Holiness theology. The church split, and Chaplain Welsh's father lost his pulpit. Through this and other tragedies, his father lost his mind. It was anguishing to Chaplain Welsh, but he grew in compassion because of how he responded with godliness to tragedy.

Evan Welsh went to Princeton Seminary and became convinced of the premillennial view as well as a place for Israel. After seminary, Evan pastored College Church and then Ward Memorial Presbyterian Church in Detroit. After pastoring at Ward, he became the chaplain at Wheaton College and during his later years there became the interim pastor of the First Hebrew Christian Church in Chicago (Presbyterian). The presbytery assigned him to churches recovering from splits or difficult situations, so he could put a salve on their pain.

Because of his favor toward me, he urged me to become the student pastor of this Hebrew Christian church when I was just twenty-four years old and still in seminary, which was how I came into the Messianic Jewish Movement. Evan Welsh impacted every area of my life and was the model by which I now understand spirituality.[9] The First Hebrew Christian Church changed its name during my pastorate to *Adat HaTikvah* (Congregation of the Hope). It was one of the Union of Messianic Jewish Congregations' founding congregations and continues to be an important congregation to this day.

I had been trained at Word of Life Camp, a dispensational organization, in eschatology and then discipled in the Reform Church in replacement theology. Therefore, I was very confused about the Last Days. I remember sitting in Dr. Welsh's living room as a new seminary student in 1970. I had been studying Revelation, I had said to myself, *It is hopeless. Nobody can ever figure this stuff out. Maybe eschatology is just conditional. If we are really good and succeed in evangelism, the terrible events of the book of Revelation will not happen. If we are really bad, it will all come.* Sometimes I had thought, partly jesting to myself, *Maybe if we believe we will get out at the beginning of the seven-year tribulation, we will, and if we do not, we will get out at the midtribulation point or after the tribulation.* Basically, I had been skeptical about the end of the Last Days. I had thought that people who taught detailed Last Days eschatology were ignorant and did not realize how difficult it was to know the truth of these things. I had tried to bypass it. I did not understand as a young seminary student at Trinity Evangelical Divinity School in Chicago that in a significant sense New Testament theology is eschatology. The Kingdom has broken in. You cannot bypass it.

I had all of these thoughts in my head when Chaplain Welsh started talking about a book he had just finished reading by George Ladd entitled *The Gospel of the Kingdom: Essays*

---

[9]   You have to have known the man to understand how impacting his life was. Thousands of people who knew him and who came to his funeral had been greatly impacted by his presence in their lives.

on the Kingdom of God in New Testament Theology. He gave me this book, and with tears in his eyes, he said to me, "The theology that my father preached is being restored to the church. I want you to read this book." I was quite touched.

I read the book and was amazed. I understood for the first time the view of the Kingdom of God that I now teach. The Kingdom has already partly come as evidenced by the Spirit, and it will come in fullness when the Messiah returns.

I also came to understand the nature of the Gospel of the Kingdom. The Gospel is an invitation to life in the Kingdom of God through Yeshua's death and Resurrection. We are now called into this Kingdom and can live in it and through it. When we live in and from the Kingdom, everything in our life is put in the right order (righteousness). It also became clear to me that there is no pretribulational rapture taught in the Bible, but that the body of believers remains until the end, fulfilling its witness to Israel and the nations. Then, the rapture occurs as part of the Second Coming of Yeshua. The presence of the body is a key to Israel being saved and would be lost if Israel is taken out of the world seven years before the end.

Many dispensationalists are rethinking theology today. It is all part of God's work to bring us together. Generally, the biggest problem with dispensational theology is the way they approach the discipline of theology. Although they claim to interpret the Bible literally, much of their support is through analogical interpretation. One example, Revelation 4:1 where John is called up to heaven is used as an analogy and a proof text of the pretribulation rapture because Revelation 4:1 is before the rapture. In addition, there is real weakness in understanding the Bible's literary genres, causing dispensationalists to interpret language literally when the biblical author does not intend this. I press for interpreting the Bible naturally according to the literary genres of the time in which it was written.

In addition, there is a pervasive pessimism in much of dispensational theology. The idea of a great world harvest at the end of the age, the Puritan hope, is not embraced. Rather they see the Church in decline. Furthermore, the Age to Come is frequently portrayed as an age in which unsaved people are ruled with a rod of iron and rebel at the end.[10] This contradicts prophecy after prophecy in the Hebrew Bible that it is an age of salvation when the knowledge of God covers the earth as the waters cover the seas. There will be great upheaval, great destruction and loss before this glorious future; however, the ultimate result will be the world's redemption.

The Latter Rain Movement

Pentecostalism continued to grow and is growing in our own day, especially in the Southern Hemisphere. The Pentecostal Movement opposed a new movement of the Spirit in the mid-twentieth century. In the late 1940s, there was an outpouring of the Spirit in Canada, which launched a movement called the Latter Rain Movement. The Latter Rain Movement was a movement where the gifts of the Spirit, especially the use of prophecy, were restored and emphasized personal prophecy in context of personal ministry. Sometimes they practiced giving direction through what was called *prophetic presbytery.* They taught fivefold ministry (apostles, prophets, evangelists, pastors, and teachers), and also understood the importance of laying hands on people.

There was a group of significant Charismatic teachers (including Derek Prince and David DuPlessis), who taught the parallel restoration of the Church and Israel. They pointed out the simultaneous timing of late nineteenth-century revivalism with early Zionism, the early Pentecostal revivals with the movement led by Hertzl, and the Latter Rain Movement and the healing revivals of the late 1940s and the early 1950s with the independence of Israel.[11] These teachers perceived God's intention to coincide spiritual visitations and

---

[10]   For a classic dipsensational theology and on this pessimism, see Louis Sperry Chafer, *Systematic Theology*, vol. 8, on Eschatology.

[11]   God did judge the Healing Movement, which was a part of the Latter Rain Movement, when leaders fell into the sins of greed and immorality, and it declined.

restorations in the Church with significant steps forward in the re-establishment of ethnic Israel in modern history. The Latter Rain Movement had worldwide influence, but Pentecostals were divided over it, and the classical denominations did not accept it. The Latter Rain Movement had significant impact on the Charismatic Movement of the 1950s and 1960s through teachers who had been influenced by or involved in the Latter Rain Movement.

There was a minor offshoot of the Latter Rain Movement in 1948 called the Manifest Sons Movement. This heresy taught that the body of believers was going to be glorified on earth before the return of the Lord. They would witness as manifest sons. Some gave up the work of evangelism to wait for their perfection.[12] This movement began to isolate itself, and unfortunately, the Latter Rain Movement unjustly came to be identified with this minor offshoot.

The Charismatic Movement

In the late 1960s, the Charismatic Movement came into full bloom. Amazingly, this worldwide movement took place at the same time God was restoring Jerusalem, paralleling the Six-Day War and the Old City of Jerusalem coming under Israeli governmental control (in 1967). Some people say Jerusalem is still trodden down because Muslims occupy the Temple Mount. Israel decided to allow that to happen.

In my senior year of high school (December 1964), I received a significant filling of the Holy Spirit through the leaders in the Dutch Reformed Church where I was a member. These leaders had been connected to the Charismatic Movement. I did not speak in tongues until some years later. It was a totally strange experience for the three weeks I was filled with the Spirit. I could not sing a hymn without tears. I was

---

[12] I believe we are to show that we are children of God but not in this sense. We should be filled with the Spirit and be holy. However, the full manifestation of our glorified bodies does not take place until the return of the Lord.

in a public high school, River Dell Senior High School, which was very oriented to secular humanism, was one of the top academic high schools in New Jersey, and had very few believers. Prior to this experience, I had always tried to witness and struggled to win classmates to the Lord. After this experience, I walked through the halls and sat in my classes as if on a cloud. I saw several students come to profess faith that year.

This move of the Holy Spirit in those days was a holy experience. People were cleaning up their lives after experiencing the Spirit and committing themselves to the study of Scripture. It was largely a movement in the context of the institutional church, as in my case within the Dutch Reformed Church. As so often happens, the establishment was fearful of the new move of the Spirit because they feared losing control. People found themselves ostracized. On the other hand, some excited Charismatics were divisive, impatient with other believers, and critical of people by focusing on whether they spoke in tongues as the basis for whether they had the Holy Spirit.[13]

Divisions came; many people in the Charismatic Movement believed that they could not live out their convictions within the existent churches' structure. The saying, "New wine cannot be put in old wineskins," was a common refrain. This is not an accurate contextual interpretation and became an excuse for the sin of schism. People started leaving their churches and forming independent Charismatic organizations, churches, and apostolic flows, which I call the new mini-denominations, under the oversight of an apostolic leader. Some of these new movements have developed a good leadership structure where the senior leader is accountable to his team or board. Others have developed a dangerous doctrine of the anointed head leader having no

---

[13] I do believe in a filling of the Spirit, and if you have had it, you know it. I believe that a person can be filled with the Holy Spirit many times. The initial time you have that experience changes your life. It is distinct. From then on you can walk in the Spirit.

accountability. In the new Charismatic groups, there was no consensus on government, accountability, or ethics. Some individuals claimed authority as God's anointed. They were not to be corrected by or accountable to anyone. Some people in independent churches were so loose that anything was accepted under the view that Christians should not judge others. They fled any connection to those who believed in any kind of authority. Others sought to form groups with balance in authority, plurality, and liberty.

The Charismatic Movement spawned the Jesus Movement. It was a tremendous movement that swept many people, especially young people, into the Kingdom. However, the spirit of lawlessness from the Anti-Vietnam War Movement and the youth culture also came into the movement. Many of the Charismatics that were saved were anti-organizational and lacked a true understanding of the body of believers. Much of the Charismatic world became either anarchistic or authoritarian.[14] There was a multiplication of independent congregations and streams. The result was a tragic fragmentation of groups that could have been unified.

Some Charismatics, as reflected in their television programs and as reported in various forms of media, have been open to every wind of doctrine. The independent Charismatics adapted an entrepreneurial and entertainment orientation. Churches were in free enterprise competition for the people who believed in Yeshua. Denominations have always been competing; however, this intensified in the Charismatic world because the loyalty to denominations and streams was at a low point and status was found in building a big church. Like the competition between Macy's and Gimbels in New York, independent Charismatic churches advertised as a way of competing. They made the competition public, saying, "Come to our

---

[14] Teaching non-accountability or the royal pastor model is a serious error. A church without standards for leaders and members is in danger of going into heresy. On the other hand, a church that supersedes conscience and the leading of the Holy Spirit and the Word (to follow leadership instead of the leading of the Holy Spirit) is also in heresy.

church. We will love you more, make you happier, and give you more for your tithe."[15]

The classical evangelicals required more in basic and moral standards for members and leaders than many of the Charismatic churches did. Understanding Church government and standards, which had been restored in the Reformation under Calvin and the Puritans, was lost. Some Charismatics believed in fivefold ministry but failed to see fivefold ministers as being elders or at least deacons in character attainment. Furthermore, they did not understand that elders were to enforce God's standards in the Church and see that loving and legitimate discipline is part of congregational life. This anarchy reflected the repudiation of the Church's denominational roots, and pride prevented them from learning from the mistakes of Church history.

If the leader had good hype and a charismatic personality, he gathered a group. Anybody who said he or she had a calling could go out and hang a shingle with himself or herself as the leader. This was without anyone in legitimate authority endorsing the person as a leader of character and to hold him or her to biblical accountability. Ordination mills were the most obvious example of this corruption. For a fee you can get a certificate and membership in the ordaining organization. Unfortunately, many of these "leaders" did not know how to disciple and care for people. As a result a tremendous moral decline was produced in the American church.

This was a fallacy of this movement. True elders must ordain true elders; this pattern can be traced in succession all the way back to the apostles. Self-appointment is not a viable alternative although a potential elder should sense his calling from God. Accountable appointment and oversight are crucial.

Discipleship Movement

Many Charismatics who saw these trends were glad to stay within their classical denominations or join Pentecostal asso-

---

[15] It is amazing how much church advertising on radio and television is toward the believer, not to the lost.

ciations. In response to these shortcomings, a group of men formed the Discipleship or Shepherding Movement. They saw a great need for order, standards, and government because of the anarchy. Some in this movement swung all the way toward a control orientation (inordinate government) and required that the shepherd approve personal decisions in a member's life.

A national hierarchy was formed. To avoid being anarchistic, some in the movement began to try to supersede the individual believer's conscience. Each level of leadership was accountable to a higher level until it reached the plurality of the top five leaders, like the structure of the Episcopal Church. This movement produced a great reaction in the rest of the Charismatic Movement. Human beings tend to swing to extremes. Today, the Discipleship Movement is fragmented, and many of the original leaders have repented; however, the problems they sought to address are still with us at a much more pronounced level.

The Word of Faith Movement

The father of the Word of Faith Movement was the late Kenneth Hagin of Rhema Bible School in Tulsa, Oklahoma. Thousands of ministers and churches around the world today still identify with this movement. It is a movement rooted in both classical Pentecostalism and the Charismatic Movement. Word of Faith reemphasized early Pentecostal beliefs as reflected in writers such as John Lake, F. F. Bosworth, Smith Wigglesworth, and Stanley Frodsham. The movement restored the view that God's promises are to be believed and received through studying, meditating on, and confessing his Word. God really meant what he said when he gave these promises.

There are many teachers in this movement of varied doctrinal maturity. We also have to understand that we are in a partial stage of Kingdom manifestation so you never attain his promises perfectly in this life.

The Word of Faith Movement does not have a good understanding of Church government. They teach a royal pastor headship model. However, a later book by Kenneth Hagin taught that ministers should be accountable in a ministerial association.[16]

Some leaders in this movement have taught a false doctrine of prosperity, defending ministers who live in sumptuous opulence. This is a tragic error and has led to unconscionable misuse of Kingdom funds, which is never a good testimony. There is, however, a promise of abundant provision for those who are generous and give to extend God's Kingdom but not for sumptuous living.

Does the Word of Faith Movement have a good understanding of other doctrines? The record is quite mixed. William DeArteaga in *Quenching the Spirit* presents a compelling evaluation. Faith is built into our lives through the Word and the certainty of God's promises of restoration. On the other hand, some of the Word of Faith teachers have no place for a Job experience. If there is a lack of healing or other failures, it is always the fault of the person individually, a kind of rugged faith individualism. Nevertheless, the Word of Faith Movement has brought an important emphasis on believing, in a straightforward way, God's promises.

The Kingdom Now Movement

The Kingdom Now Movement is an offshoot of the Charismatic Movement. Many of these people were Pentecostal in their pre-Charismatic days. Some have misrepresented this movement as teaching replacement theology, but this is only true of a minority. The Kingdom Now Movement is a movement of Charismatics who discovered Reform theology. Because Reform theology had significant replacement proponents, some Kingdom Now people are replacement, but most are amillennial, some are postmillennial, and some are premillennial.

---

[16]   From an oral lecture in 1982—the CD is available at www.rhema.org—"The Gifts and Calling of God."

When criticism is directed at an aspect of the movement, some conclude that the movement must be completely without value. We find good and bad in all evangelical movements. Kingdom Now proponents need to see the place of Israel in the Last Days and study the Puritans of the seventeenth century who believed in a future for Israel.

The Vineyard Movement

John Wimber, the head of the Vineyard Movement, had a profound effect in the American church world and significantly but secondarily in Britain and continental Europe. Making the theology of George Ladd the theological foundation for understanding the Kingdom, Wimber added the role of signs and wonders as key manifestations of the established but not fully manifested Kingdom. Wimber has influenced countless evangelicals to embrace the Holy Spirit's gifts and power.

The Vineyard is trying to combine a seriousness of evangelical doctrine with the Charismatic experience. This movement does not endorse tongues as the essential sign of the baptism of the Spirit, which has produced significant openings. Scholarship is combined with spiritual power. The one great weakness in the Vineyard is a lack of clarity in membership standards: If you participate, then you are a member, but if you do not, you are not. A classical commitment to membership standards is crucial in establishing a real covenant and in being able to enforce church discipline. American courts allow for Church discipline only if there is a clear membership covenant. However, recently the Vineyard Movement has been progressing toward clear leadership standards.

Leading evangelical scholars (Wayne Grudem of Trinity, Peter Wagner of Fuller, Jack Deere formerly of Dallas Theological Seminary, and the late John White, the noted Christian psychiatrist) have written in support of the Vineyard Movement.

Summary

We see then that the nineteenth and twentieth centuries produced both restorations of truth and fragmentations. A great focus among Protestants in spreading the Gospel restored the first-century emphasis on Kingdom extensions, which had been lacking in Protestant Movements. Movements to empower the laity and to embrace the gifts of the Spirit and the visible evidence of the Spirit's work in healings, signs, and wonders were important developments. The emphasis on the restoration of Israel also became a consensus in the English-speaking Christian world in the nineteenth century, and this emphasis continued through the twentieth century. There were also movements that embraced the importance of the ministry leaders functioning according to Ephesians 4:11 ff.

My greatest concern today is to see an end to fragmentation and an increase in accountability and standards for leaders. To be effective, leaders must be supported in an intercongregational and interdenominational way. From the example of Count Zinzendorf in the eighteenth century to leaders in our own day, I have hope that this can happen. However, this quest for biblical unity has not yet become a consensus among leaders in the Church and Messianic Jewish worlds.

7

The Church World Today

There is still a Charismatic contingent in the older denominations, which continues to be significant. Moreover, there has been tremendous growth in independent churches of all sizes. There is also the new cell church emphasis affecting many through the teaching of David Cho, Ralph Neighbor Jr., Dale Galloway, Carl George, and others.

There are many forms of the cell church philosophy, including small groups within larger congregations, house churches, and the G12 Movement. Discipling groups of twelve, called the G12 Movement and based in South America, is an important development. The philosophy of these groups is based on the long-term covenant relationships of G12 group members. G12 groups are encouraged to last for many years. In this model G12 groups replace other forms of house groups and cell groups.

A new house church movement is also important. In Europe the house churches represent a fresh approach to the intimacy and discipleship that reach many who do not find fulfillment in traditional church models. Successful house churches are generally linked by apostolic and prophetic leadership. In places like China, the house church that meets underground has multiplied into tens of millions.

There is continued numerical decline in mainline denominations in the West, but the Southern Hemisphere is now by far the locale of vibrant, growing Christian movements.[1] God

---

[1] While I am concerned about these problems, sometimes God will use the problems and the decline to wake people up to what he wants.

is not in favor of competing denominations and streams, which cause fragmentation of the body. He is not calling for apostolic streams and denominations whose congregations are isolated from one another and are loyal only to their stream or denomination. The franchised and independent say, "Come and buy my product because it is better than the product of the church down the street." Within those types of churches, there is this attitude: "Come to us, we have sound doctrine. Come here, and you will be healed. Come here because we are more entertaining. Come here for what we have got in our children's program." The nature of Church life at the end of the twentieth century is multiple denominations and apostolic flows without interaccountability, prayer, or cooperative effort.

Thank God there are some great exceptions. The Christian public needs to be educated out of its biblical naiveté. Many churches use radio to draw the Christian public. Yet in all of this the Church is not winning the lost in the West. The money spent on media for evangelism—there is a place for media— could be better spent on evangelism in the local church. Ninety percent of those who receive the Lord do so by the witness of a friend. In China where there is no freedom of religion, the Church is growing by leaps and bounds and demonstrates powerful signs and mighty wonders.

Indications of Hope

There are signs of hope. I believe it is God's intention to unify all true believers in the power of the Holy Spirit and bring all of the truths of restoration together in the end.

First, there are the cell churches, G12 churches, and other new small group church models. In cell churches, you do not go to church to only be served by the product offered. You become part of a community, accountable to a cell and equipped to be effective to witness to lost people. Some megachurches are great service centers but do not build community. People who are built into community and who serve each other effectively do not easily switch to become part of another church.

Biblically, the idea of membership in the church is not about going to hear good messages (this can be done by television or CDs); it is where you build into community and accountability and get equipped to do ministry work. The cell meetings are considered more important than the larger gatherings. The elders and spouses are accountable to each other; they oversee cell or small group leaders and model what they teach. Cell congregations are more secure about their membership and tend to be more cooperative with other area congregations. The larger meeting is a celebration, but the gifts of the Spirit, as in the meetings in 1 Corinthians 14, are more operative in the smaller cell group setting. This is one of the great waves of the future Church. Successful cell leaders become overseers of several cells. Overseers of cells become new missionaries and congregation planters. In this model, Bible college and seminary can function in an adjunct capacity to on-the-job training. This is a true biblical restoration.

The second great indication of hope is new value of unity among leaders and churches in various cities. David DuPlessis began to work toward this end, and men, such as Francis Frangipane, John Dawson, Ed Silvoso, Dutch Sheets, and Chuck Pierce, have powerfully made the case for coming together in integrity, love, prayer, and cooperative unity in every locality. I believe that God wants to gather us together in each place and break down the walls of competition and fear. We need to seek the heart of the Lord for unity crossdenominationally. This is happening in Cedar Rapids, Kansas City, California, Nashville, Baltimore, Harrisburg, and in other cities in significant ways.

Such unity should not destroy ethnicity or a distinctive call for the Jews. Unity was Yeshua's great prayer and may be the last great stage in restoration. In the unity described in John 17 the Church will be given a heart to overcome its competition and join together in mutual accountability and cooperation across denominational and apostolic lines through the acceptance of the Holy Spirit's power, which will break down the barriers. True unity will include moral and doctrinal foundations of stability, mutual support in disciplinary situations, and a recognized intercongregational leadership in the local region. Without this, any move toward unity will be only transient.

In the Last Days our various competing apostolic flows and denominations will decrease with centrality, and the Lord will raise up the unified in each city's body of believers to greater centrality. The Church of the City, the idea of one leadership structure for each city, will increase in frequency. As John the Baptist said, "He must increase, and I must decrease." So also the Church as seen in John 17 must increase, and our competing denominations and lack of standards must decrease as God raises up a unified Church that has within it the truths of all of the past restoration movements. This implies a board principle of leadership succession where mature true elders (leaders) ordain new elders. Senior elders are recognized in the city's council (presbytery).

Finally, the Church will also recover an appreciation and self-understanding of its Jewish roots. It will make room for a Jewish expression. Jewish members of other churches will be encouraged to be Jewish for the Church's enrichment. There is an important place for encouraging the saved remnant of Israel. By regaining unity, the Church will see that its capstone to victory is the salvation of Israel. The Church will see through prayer and mercy, they will help establish as a central part of its calling the saved remnant of Israel. This will lead to all of Israel being saved.

The Emerging Church Movement emphasizes many of these themes and gives great hope for the Western Church. However, it still has to convey the importance of the Jewish people. One of their leading thinkers, Alan Hirsch, is Jewish and has this burden.[2] In places like China, the descrip-

---

2   Alan Hirsch, *The Forgotten Ways* (Grand Rapids: Brazos Press, 2006).

tion of the Church given reflects the Church here and is the only kind of Church they know! Philip Jenkins's great writings on *The Next Christendom* show the promise of Southern Global Christianity, where a Book of Acts mentality of power, signs, wonders, supernaturalism, and more is the common orientation.

World missions and making Israel jealous is the two-pronged Church mission in every age. The restoration of Jewish roots of understanding is part of the unification and a key to transcending the many exisitng divisions. Will we find unity by becoming more Presbyterian, Baptist, or Pentecostal? No. Further progress will come from a more accurate biblical context for understanding our Jewish roots.

What are the key dimensions of Jewish roots to be restored? First, gentile churches do not need to look like Messianic Jewish synagogues. Christianity reflects aspects that are a legitimate contextualization of truth in gentile cultures. To conform the Church to the whole of Torah and seek to make churches into Messianic Jewish synagogues in expression is a mistake.

However, key aspects of those Jewish roots are important. First, the Greek influences on Christianity will be rescinded for original Jewish thought. God is understood as a living, involved, and passionate Being and not an abstract, timeless, unmoved, and unaffected god as in Greek thought. The Church embraces the value of God's creation and life in the real-time world. Also, it will not split over concerns for abstractions in interpretation (a very Greek orientation that has also influenced rabbinic Judaism). Rather the Church will embrace the broad and clear assertions of the Bible. This includes the broader functional definitions of the deity of Yeshua and God in his triunity and more.

Second, the body of believers accepts some central doctrine of early Judiasm. The correct regard for the Law and a healthy understanding of Law and grace is restored. The Church also will develop a functional eschatology where believers and Israel are the actors on the stage of eschatological

cal history. There will be less speculation on end time details when the nature of first-century Jewish apocalyptic literature is understood.

Third, the Church should understand itself as organically connected to the Jewish people through its connection to the Jewish Messiah Yeshua and the Messianic Jewish community. It supports living Jewish believers and the Church's alignment with the Jewish people and with Messianic Jews through an understanding of the importance of the feasts for teaching.

Generally, most aspects of restoration are a return to Jewish roots in understanding. It may look like we've become fragmented, carnal, and nonaccountable; however, people will become disgusted with the present situation in the West and will seek something higher. They may enter into something better than what the Church has yet been. The Holy Spirit can open the eyes of leaders in the Church all over the world.

8

Conclusion

We have seen an amazing history of restoration since the Reformation with even the Catholic Church reformed as a result of these restorations. However, it has been two steps forward and one step back. Messianic Jews now take heart in the official Catholic repudiation of replacement theology and their firm assertion of the continued election of ethnic Jewry. This was the key affirmation in the Vatican II document *Nostre Aetate*. It is now clearly enshrined in the New Catholic Catchecism, where Israel's coming to faith in the Messiah is seen as a key to world redemption.

As part of this change in the Catholic Church, a contingent of Messianic Jewish leaders have become part of a significant informal dialogue with leading churchmen that is supported by the Vatican. One Catholic archdeacon, under the oversight of his cardinal archbishop, oversees scores of ecumenical Charismatic communities. These communities have committed themselves to Israel's restoration. They also host unifying events in various cities. I am still deeply concerned by some Catholic extra biblical teaching. However, if the Catholic Church can so positively change and become a pro-Jewish church, we can trust that God can bring further change to the rest of the Church.

When reviewing Church history as a whole, earlier movements anticipated later restorations. Luther restored faith and scripture. In the Reform and Puritan movements, biblical church government was restored. The Puritans had a special love for the Jewish people. The Reform also brought a biblical understanding to vocation and culture, demonstrating the principles of the Kingdom in all realms of life. The Lutheran Pietists and Moravians emphasized prayer, holiness, and world missions. They had a significant heart for Jewish people and their salvation. The Moravians prayed for one hundred years at Hernhutt, birthing modern missions. In the Methodists, small group accountability and sanctification were restored to higher levels. Historic revivals were great leaps forward. The Anabaptists and Baptists restored immersion baptism for adults. The Holiness Movement (Finney, Moody, Murray, and Torrey) restored a deeper life walk. They began the healing movement at the end of the nineteenth century. The Pentecostal Movement restored greater clarity on the gifts of the Spirit and the use of the gift of tongues. The Latter Rain Movement restored the place of prophecy, the laying on of hands for spiritual gifts, and fivefold ministry.

Later restorations were amazingly parallel to God's work in restoring the nation of Israel. Early Zionism paralleled the Holiness Movement. The movement of Hertz's Zionist Jewish Congress corresponded with the early Pentecostal Movement. The independence of Israel ran simultaneous to the Latter Rain Movement and the healing revival of the late 1940s and early 1950s. The capture of the old city of Jerusalem in 1967 occurred during the early Charismatic Movement and the Jesus Movement. This was the time of the birth of the modern Messianic Jewish Movement, too.

Today, we look for a new revival and restoration. We see it in some other parts of the world more than in America. It is a move toward John 17's unity, prayer, holiness, and accountability in every locality. Its success will be the concern of every legitimate New Covenant congregation, lead to recovering a Jewish-rooted understanding of the Church, and affirm the legitimacy of the saved remnant of Israel. This is not yet true of the majority of churches, but it is in a significant and growing minority.

In the Last Days a restored body of believers with its Jewish members will make Israel jealous. All Israel will be saved. Yeshua will return, deliver Israel, and establish his worldwide Kingdom. Finally, Messianic Jews are very quick to point out the danger of arrogance in the Church. Rightly, Paul, in Romans 11, warns against gentile arrogance and reminds his readers that the root supports them and they do not support the root. Our people will be grafted in again, but our temptation is to look at the worst parts of Church history and too easily dismiss the historic Church as irrelevant to us. Some accuse the historic Church of being pagan when much of its practice has merely contextualized the Gospel. There are pagan elements that can be criticized but not so simplistically and inaccurately. Claims that Church symbols are pagan are misleading when a symbol's or ritual's meaning is its understanding as set by the community that practices it. The historic Church has brought great advances to humanity. Through it the Scriptures have come to the world and the New Covenant Scriptures have been preserved for centuries.

Correction is in order; however, this correction is in a context of empathetic appreciation where possible. Arrogance against the Church must be avoided because it is the godly of the Church who have passed on the deepest reflections on the meaning of Yeshua's life, death, and resurrection. This obviously cannot be found in classical Judaism. The Messianic Jewish Movement has added new perspectives to understanding Yeshua that the Church is benefitting from. Messianic Jews are called to honor that which is good and right in the Church, to learn from its leaders, and to benefit from the study of the Church's teachings, liturgy, traditions, and hymnology. If we do this, we will be astonished at the treasures awaiting us because it will enhance the development of Messianic Jewish tradition and expression. If Messianic Judaism is to mature, it will not happen without a deeper appreciation of the Church, as well as its own Jewish heritage. And, if the Church is to fulfill its calling, it must embrace Israel, the Jewish people and Messianic Judaism.

APPENDIX

In 1995 a project for aligning the Church with the Messianic Jewish Congregational Movement was launched. It was called Toward Jerusalem Council II. This name reflects the view that the Church needs to affirm the calling of Messianic Jews to identify and live as Jews. Our committee includes Protestant, Catholic, Orthodox Christian, and Messianic Jewish members. Our goal is parallel to the first-century Messianic Jews releasing Gentiles from Jewish life in Acts 15. Many have called this the Jerusalem Council.

This project was not a publicized effort. The sensitivity of diplomacy made that necessary. We sponsored prayer journeys that took our committee with other supporters to the locations of church councils that included anti-Jewish and anti-Messianic Jewish canons. Dialogue has taken place with the highest echelons of some of the churches, including the Roman Catholic Church and Anglican Church.

In the fall of 2006 in Jerusalem, Toward Jerusalem Council II sponsored a prayer convocation in Jerusalem that included every major stream of the Church and representatives from every continent. This convocation issued a call to the churches. From this call a set of declarations was embraced and recommended for adoption by all churches and ministry organizations. This important document is reproduced below. It is an important statement of restoration.

The Seven Affirmations

Consistent with the principle established in the original Jerusalem Council of Acts Chapter 15 regarding respect for diversity in the Body of Christ concerning Jewish and gentile

identity, we _____ do make the
following affirmations:

1. We affirm the election of Israel, its irrevocable nature, and
   God's unfinished work with the Jewish people regarding salvation and the role of Israel as a blessing to the nations.
2. We affirm that Jews who come to faith in the Messiah,
   Yeshua, are called to retain their Jewish identity and live
   as part of their people in ways consistent with the New
   Covenant.
3. We affirm the formation of Messianic Jewish congregations as a significant and effective way to express Jewish
   collective identity (in Yeshua) and as a means of witness-
   ing of Yeshua to the Jewish community. We also affirm
   Jewish individuals and groupings which are part of
   churches and encourage them in Jewish life and identity.
4. We affirm our willingness as an ecclesiastical body to
   build bridges to the Messianic Jewish community, to extend the hand of friendship, and to pray for their growth
   and vitality.
5. We affirm our willingness to share our resources with
   Messianic Jewish congregations, mission organizations,
   and theological training institutes so as to empower them
   to fulfill their God-given purpose.
6. We affirm our willingness to be a voice within our own
   ecclesiastical structures and spheres of influence against
   all forms of antisemitism, replacement theology (super-
   cessionism), and teaching that precludes the expression of
   Jewish identity in Yeshua.
7. Finally, we affirm that as Jewish and gentile expressions
   of life in Yeshua grow organically side by side with distinct identities that God will be glorified, that the Kingdom of Heaven will be advanced, and that the vision of
   "the one new man" in Ephesians 2 will unfold as part of
   the original Abrahamic blessing to the nations.

Bibliography

Bainton, Roland. *Here I Stand.* New York: Pierce and Smith, 1950.

Brown, Michael L. *Our Hands are Stained with Blood.* Shippensburg: Destiny Image, 1992.

Burgess, Stanely M. and Eduard M. Van Der Mass. *The Dictionary of Pentecostal and Charismatic Movements.* Grand Rapids: Zondervan, 2002.

Chadwick, Henry. *The Early Church.* New York: Penguin, 1989.

Chadwick, Owen. *The Reformation.* New York: Penguin, 1990.

Davies, W. D. *Paul and Rabbinic Judaism.* Mifflentown: Sigler Press, 1980.

Gurnell, William. *The Christian in Complete Armour.* Chicago: Moody, 1999.

Jenkins, Phillip. *The Next Christendom.* New York: Oxford University Press, 2002.

Kelly, J. N. D. *Early Christian Doctrine.* New York: Harper Collins, 1978.

Kobler, Franz. *The Vision Was There.* London: World Jewish Congress, 1954.

Ladd, George. *The Gospel of the Kingdom.* Grand Rapids: Eerdmans, 1959.

Lauterette, Kenneth Scott. *A History of the Expansion of Christianity.* New York: Harper and Brothers, 1945.

Murray, Ian. *The Puritan Hope.* London: Banner of Truth, 1971.

Parkes, James. *The Conflict of the Church and the Synagogue.* New York: Herron Press, 1974.

Weinlick, John R., *Count Zinzendorf.* Bethleham: Moravian Press, 1989.

Other Related Books from Messianic Jewish Publishers
Available through Messianic Jewish Resources Int'l
www.messianicjewish.net
1-800-410-7367

Jewish New Testament   *Dr. David H. Stern*
The New Testament is a Jewish book, written by Jews, initially
for Jews. Its central figure was a Jew. His followers were all Jews;
yet no other version really communicates its original, essential
Jewishness. This version uses neutral terms and Hebrew names.
Highlights Jewish references. Corrects mistranslation from anti-
Jewish theological bias.
Hardback   JB02 $19.99   20 CD's JC01 $49.99
Paperback JB01 $14.99   MP3   JC02 $49.99

Jewish New Testament Commentary   *Dr. David H. Stern*
This companion to the Jewish New Testament enhances Bible
study. Passages and expressions are explained in their original
cultural context.
Hardback   JB06 $34.99
Paperback JB10 $29.99

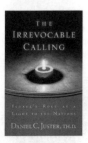

The Irrevocable Calling   *Daniel C. Juster, Th.D.*
Israel's Role As A Light To The Nations
Referring to the chosen-ness of the Jewish people, Paul, the
Apostle, wrote "For God's free gifts and his calling are irrevocable" (Rom. 11:29). This messenger to the Gentiles understood
the unique calling of his people, Israel. Expands Paul's words,
showing how Israel was uniquely chosen to bless the world and
how these blessings can be enjoyed today.
LB66 $8.99

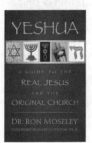

Yeshua   *Dr. Ron Moseley*
A Guide to the Real Jesus and the Original Church
Dr. Ron Moseley opens up the history of the Jewish roots of the
Christian faith. He illuminates the Jewish background of Yeshua
and the Church and never flinches from his purpose—to show
"Jesus was a Jew who was born, lived, and died, within first cen-
tury Judaism."
LB29 $12.99

Other Related Books continued

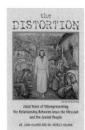

The Distortion   *Dr. John Fischer and Dr. Patrice Fischer*
2000 Years of Misrepresenting the Relationship Between Jesus
the Messiah and the Jewish People
Did the Jews kill Jesus? Did they really reject him? With the rise
of global anti-semitism, it is important to understand what the
Gospels teach about the relationship between Jewish people and
their Messiah.
LB54 $11.99

Restoring the Jewishness of the Gospely   *Dr. David H. Stern*
A Message to Christians
This classic work by David H. Stern, Ph.D. introduces Christians
to the Jewish roots of their faith, challenges some conventional
ideas, and raises some neglected questions.
LB70 $9.99

God's Appointed Times   *Rabbi Barney Kasdan, M. Div.*
A Practical Guide for Understanding and
Celebrating the Biblical Holidays
The biblical holy days—Passover, Firstfruits, Tabernacles, etc.—
can be a source of God's blessing for all believers—Jew and
Gentile—today. This book includes the historical background,
traditional Jewish observance, New Testament relevance, and
prophetic significance of each biblical holiday, plus music, crafts
and holiday recipes.
LB63 $12.99

Fire on the Mountain   *Dr. Louis Goldberg*
Past Renewals, Present Revivals and the Coming Return of Israel
The term "revival" is often used to describe a person or congregation turning to God. Is this something that "just happens," or
can it be brought about? Dr. Louis Goldberg, author and former
professor of Hebrew and Jewish Studies at Moody Bible Institute,
examines real revivals that took place in Bible times and applies
them to today.
LB38 $15.99